Marcus Lafayette Byrn

The Artist and Tradesman's Companion

Marcus Lafayette Byrn

The Artist and Tradesman's Companion

ISBN/EAN: 9783743394506

Manufactured in Europe, USA, Canada, Australia, Japa

Cover: Foto ©Suzi / pixelio.de

Manufactured and distributed by brebook publishing software (www.brebook.com)

Marcus Lafayette Byrn

The Artist and Tradesman's Companion

THE ARTIST AND TRADESMAN'S COMPANION;

EMBRACING THE MANUFACTURE AND THE APPLICATION OF VARNISHES TO PAINTING AND OTHER BRANCHES OF THE ARTS; INSTRUCTIONS FOR WORKING ENAMEL, FOIL, ETC.; THE ART OF GLAZING, IMITATION OF GOLD COLOR, TORTOISE-SHELL, MARBLE, AND ART OF STAINING WOOD AND METAL; IMITATION OF FANCY WOODS, GRANITE, PRECIOUS STONES, SILVER, BRASS AND COPPER; HOUSE-PAINTING, CARRIAGE-PAINTING, ETC., WITH EVERYTHING RELATING TO THE FINE ARTS, ETC. ETC., ENTIRELY SIMPLIFIED.

With Illustrations.

COMPILED BY M. LAFAYETTE BYRN, M. D.,

GRADUATE OF THE UNIVERSITY OF THE CITY OF NEW YORK.

Author of "The Complete Practical Brewer," "Detection of Fraud and Protection of Health," "The Complete Practical Distiller," &c. &c.

PHILADELPHIA:
J. B. LIPPINCOTT & CO.
1866.

ENTERED, according to Act of Congress, in the Year One Thousand Eight Hundred and Fifty-three, by STEARNS & COMPANY, in the Clerk's Office of the District Court of the United States, for the Southern District of New York.

PREFACE.

This little work has been prepared with great care, for the purpose of making it practically useful to a large class of persons engaged almost entirely in pursuits of this nature, and also to aid any and every one in performing such duties in the arts as will usually be needed, where an experienced artist cannot be found; as is the case very often in that portion of this country, where the arts and sciences have not made such progress as we witness in the older settled parts, as the eastern and middle states.

Everything has been so simplified, that a boy fifteen years old can perform nearly all the operations in a short time, by a little care and attention, with credit to himself and at a comparative small outlay of means. It is hoped that the effort made to render this book of great service to every practical man throughout this country, will prove successful; if so, the grand object in its preparation will have been attained.

All the works on this subject have been made use of attainable, and the matter has been appropriated to the best purpose in the present volume.

M. La B.

CONTENTS.

	PAGE.
THE MANUFACTURE OF VARNISH on a large scale	15
OF AN ALEMBIC, OR STILL, suitable for the manufacture of Varnish	32
To make Red Sealing Wax	41
To make Black Sealing Wax	41
To make Artificial Venice Turpentine	42
To make French Polish	44
To make Artificial Asphaltum	45
To make Black Varnish of Silhet	45
To make Varnish of Caoutchouc	45
To make Varnish for Balloons	46
Caoutchouc Varnish, with Naphtha	46
To make Brunswick Black	47
To make Black Japan Varnish	47
To make White Hard Varnish	47
To make Sheldrake's Copal Varnish	48
To make Shellac Varnish	48
DIVISION OF VARNISHES into Five Classes, with Instructions for Preparing them, &c	49
Class First.—Varnishes possessing a Drying Quality, made with Rectified Spirit of Wine	49

CONTENTS.

	PAGE
Class Second.—Varnishes which, though Spirituous, are less Drying than Class First	51
Class Third of Varnishes	57
Class Fourth.—Varnishes of Copal, made with Ether and Oil of Turpentine	64
DESCRIPTION OF A FURNACE, intended for the Liquefaction of Copal and Amber	68
Class Fifth of Varnishes	72
OF THE VARIOUS COLORED VARNISHES, with Instructions for Preparing them.—Glazing on Metallic or other substances.—Preparation of Foils, &c.	77
Transparent Green	77
Another Green Color	77
Another Green Color, by Composition	77
Blue Color	78
Superb Liquid Blue	78
Yellow	80
Dark Red	80
Violet	80
OBSERVATIONS ON THE APPLICATION OF COPAL VARNISH, for Repairing Opaque Enamel	82
White, Black, Yellow,	84
Blue, Green, Red, Purple, Brick-Red, Buff-Color, Violet, Pearl Gray	85
Preparation of Foil	86
Blue Color	88
Green	88
Red	88
Lilac	90
Ruby Color	90
Rose Color	90

CONTENTS.

	PAGE.
Poppy Red	90
Plum Color	90

Of the Process for Preparing Waxed or Varnished Cloth, Varnished Silk, Court-Plaster, Various Methods of Staining Wood, &c.	91
Fine Printed Varnished Cloth	94
Varnished Silk	95
Another kind of Varnished Silk	99
Court-Plaster	99
Numerous Processes for Staining Wood	101
A Red Stain	101
A Light Red, approaching to Pink	101
A very Dark-Red Stain	101
The old Method of Staining Wood Red	102
A Yellow Stain	102
Blue Stains	102
A Blue Stain with Copper	103
A Green Stain	103
A Blue Stain with Indigo	103
A Purple Stain	104
A Black Stain	104
A very fine Black	105
A common Black Stain	105
Mahogany Stains	105
A Light Red-Brown Mahogany	105
Spanish Mahogany Stain	106
Fancy Woods	106
Rose Wood Stains	106
Observations on House-Painting, with Instructions for Preparing the various Colors, &c.	108
Tinting	117

CONTENTS.

	PAGE
Gilding in Oil	118
Of Compound Colors	119
Brilliant Peach Blossom	120
Lilac, Light Gray, French Gray, Orange Color, Buff, Green	122
Straw Color in Size	123
Blue in Distemper.—Blue Verditer	123
Drab in Size	124
Milk-Paint for In-door Work	124
Distemper Colors for Walls	125
Lime Whitewash.—Paste for Paper-hanging.—To Imitate Cherry-Tree	127
Transparent Colors for Painting.—Directions for Inside Painting	128
The Second Coat for White.—The Third Coat.—Painting in Dead-Colors for Inside Work	129
To Flat a French Gray on Hard Finished Walls	130
To make and apply the Flatting	131
Instructions for Writing	132
To give Lustre to a Light Blue Ground.—Harmony of Colors.—Marbling Paper	134
To Prepare the Ground for the Oak-Rollers.—Oil for Graining Oak.—Spirit Graining for Oak	139
To Imitate Oak in Distemper	142
To Imitate Old Oak.—To Grain Oak in Distemper	144
To Imitate Old Oak in Oil.—Pollard Oak in Distemper.—To Imitate Pollard Oak	145
Pollard Oak in Oil	146
A good Ground for Mahogany.—To Imitate Mottled Mahogany	147
To Imitate New Mahogany.—To Imitate Rose Wood with Rollers	148
To Imitate Bird's-eye Maple	150

	PAGE.
To Imitate Curled Maple	151
Curled Maple, in Oil, for Outside Work	152
Satin Wood	153
To Imitate Yew Tree.—To Imitate Hair Wood	154
Hair Wood for Chairs.—To Imitate Black and Gold Marble	155
Dove Marble	157
White-Veined Marble	159
Sienna Marble	160
Italian Marble	161
Red Marble, Jasper Marble, Blue and Gold Marble	162
Imitation of Marble in Distemper	163
Verd-antique	165
Marble to resemble Jasper.—To Imitate Porphyry Marble	168
To Imitate Granite.—To Polish Woods and Marbles	170
To Imitate Tortoise-Shell	171
Varnish for Applying on Glass.—Water-proof Polish.—To Heighten the Color of Gold on Brass	172
To Dissolve Gold	172
Instructions for Gilding the edges of Paper	174
General Observations on the Art of Gilding	175
MISCELLANEOUS	184
Art of Imitating Oak, Mahogany, Satin Wood, Walnut, Rose Wood, and Maple	200
Directions for Painting Sail-Cloth, to make it Pliant, Water-proof, and Durable	214
Directions for making a Varnish which will protect Glass from the rays of the sun	214

ARTIST AND TRADESMAN'S COMPANION.

THE

ARTIST AND TRADESMAN'S COMPANION.

THE MANUFACTURE OF VARNISH ON AN EXTENSIVE SCALE.

It is to the resinous and gum-resinous substances, more particularly, that we are indebted for the best varnish; though the pure gums, isinglass, the white of eggs, and a few other substances, may become ingredients in varnish sometimes. The principal liquids used as vehicles for varnish, are spirit of wine, the essential oils extracted by distillation from vegetables and the fixed or fat oils. The essential qualities of most varnishes are transparency, limpidity, and lustre. It is necessary, though, that they should possess the quality of drying speedily, and giving solidity to the resinous stratum which serves as a glazing to the bodies which they cover. It is also requisite that a composition of this sort should at the same time be colorless, so that it will not weaken or disfigure the tints of the colors which it covers, and which it ought, on the contrary, to bring out in their full brightness, by protecting them from the influence of air and moisture.

Gum sandarac, employed formerly by the Arabs for

this purpose, was the only matter which seemed likely to answer the proposed end. It is easily prepared, and possesses lustre; but it is attended with the disadvantage of a little dryness, which may be corrected. Turpentine, and all the modifications of it by the effect of evaporation; mastic, which has more solidity than sandarac; gum anime, and gum elemi, gum lac and copal, compose nearly the catalogue of the matters employed for the composition of drying varnishes, or those made with spirit of wine.

The extreme dryness of some of them is corrected by uniting them with others which are less dry, and which still retain a portion of essential oil, such as gum elemi, gum anime, camphor, and turpentine. The same effect is produced also by substituting, instead of spirit of wine, a less dry fluid, such as the oil of turpentine. Experience has set bounds to the number of the liquids proper for serving as vehicles in the composition of varnish. The nature of spirit of wine was suited to light drying and colorless compositions, when artists were desirous to correct the strong odor which accompanies most varnishes. In examining the essential oils, artists must have first distinguished those which, on account of their lightness, seemed to exhibit intermediate qualities between spirits of wine and oils of the greatest consistence; hence the use of oil of turpentine, and oil of lavender. Oil of turpentine gives to varnish more body than spirits of wine; it might, indeed, be substituted in all cases for it, if the strong odor it emits were not, to some persons, a cause for rejecting it.

For varnishes designed to be applied to ceilings, wainscoting, and furniture, it is far superior, because it renders them equally brilliant, and gives them more durability. During the summer, in particular, this odor is soon destroyed; and if the artist takes care to employ a spirit varnish for the last coat, there will be no odor at all. The use of essential oil of lavender is more applicable to delicate oil painting than to the art of the varnisher.

Though naturally dryer, next to oil of turpentine, than other essential oils, it is still too fat and unctuous for varnishes. It may be introduced in small quantities in the composition of varnishes made with spirit of wine and oil of turpentine, when it is necessary to lessen their drying quality, or when metallic colors are used in the state of pure oxides. The other essential oils known in commerce are either too dear, or too fat, or too much colored, to form part of the liquors for the solution of resins. The number of fat or fixed oils useful to art is as much limited as that of the essential or volatile oils. Oil of white poppy seed, nut oil, and linseed oil, are the only ones found by experience to be fit for the composition of fat varnishes, when they have undergone preliminary preparations which deprive them of their unctuous quality, and render them drying.

Oil of olives, being without much color, would answer the purpose of the artist better than nut oil or linseed oil, which are always colored, if it did not possess an unctuous matter, which can be removed only by destroying a part of the oil itself. The case is the same with oil of turnips and oil of hemp-seed; and the processes to which the seeds of the beech-tree are subjected before the oil is expressed from them, give it a red color, which renders it unfit for varnish. To judge, then, from the results alone, varnishes are nothing but solutions of pure resins, or resinous gums, in an appropriate spirituous or oily liquid.

Acid liquors, therefore, and alkaline liquors, though the latter have the property of combining with oils and with resins, and of reducing them to the saponaceous state, are in no case endowed with the essential qualities requisite for the composition of varnishes. If saline, acid, and alkaline liquors, considered as solvents, are incapable of answering the views of the varnisher; water, a simple substance, without odor, and almost without savor, is no less contrary to them. It is the nature of resins to resist its action. Water also has the property of uniting with the spirit of wine, which holds a resin in solution, and of precipitating the latter under the form of a white powder. These effects require the most scrupulous attention on the part of the artist, in regard to the choice of the spirit he intends to employ in his composition.

The best brandy, and even spirit superior to brandy, if of greater specific gravity than 0·835, are unfit for making varnish. The water which such liquors contain is an obstacle to the solution of resins; and it precipitates the resinous portions which the spirituous part has been able to dissolve by the aid of heat. The solution is turbid, and difficult of clarification. Some resins should be washed before they are employed in the composition of varnish.

Mastic, sandarac, and even copal itself, which is divided into small portions, &c., require previous washing, which is attended by no kind of inconvenience. The case would be the same with amber, were not this precaution rendered useless by the process to which it is subjected. These resins are immersed in water after the fine powder has been separated from them by a hair-sieve. The fragments and resinous tears are then rubbed between the hands to detach the dust, the lighter parts, and the fragments of bark. These separated parts float on the surface; and, in consequence of their lightness, afford the means of removing them with facility. The washed resin is then spread out on a piece of linen cloth, or a hair-sieve, which is covered with a sheet of paper, and the whole is exposed to a current of air to dissipate the moisture.

Resins washed in this manner, and well dried, are much fitter for the composition of varnishes than those which have not been subjected to the same operation. A few more precautions are still necessary in composing delicate varnishes, such as those designed for valuable paintings and other objects of luxury. It will be proper to separate the pure resinous tears from those which are stained, or which are accompanied with portions of the bark of the tree that produced them.

Some resins are much more soluble in spirit than others. The goodness of the varnish depends not only on the choice of the soluble matters, but also on the state of the liquors in which they are to be dissolved. A varnish may be of an inferior quality, though the vehicle has dissolved as much resin as it can take up. The excellence of spirit of wine cannot be determined merely by the light; and for this reason, the best means have been enlarged on, as a guide to the artist and amateur on this point, which is of the utmost importance. It may be stated, however, that it is scarcely possible to determine accurately when any fixed or essential oil is quite pure. If an essential oil has a fat oil mixed with it, as the first is usually soluble in rectified spirit of wine—if, on being poured into the spirit, it does not dissolve in it, but makes the spirit foul, and leaves ultimately a gross sediment, we may be certain that the essential oil has been adulterated.

But there does not exist any known method of proving definitely when one essential oil is mixed with another, as is sometimes the case with oil of lavender, that being occasionally deteriorated with oil of rosemary, except by its altered or impure smell; nor is the difficulty less with fat or expressed oils. If, however, an essential oil is diluted with rectified spirit of wine, as it sometimes is, when such diluted oil is poured into water, the whole mixture will become turbid, and more or less milky.

With these facts before us, such are the guides in which the artist ought to place confidence in regard to the composition of varnish; by these alone he can hope to obtain success. But whatever efforts may be made to produce a maximum of solution in the mixture of the matters, he can attain only to a point of saturation proportioned to the nature of the resins, and to the present state of the liquors employed. The art, however, is still imperfect, if the practical part be confined merely to the choice of the substances. Too great a number of them, as well as too great proportions, will disappoint the artist in his expectations. By simplifying the compositions, and reducing them to a small number of substances, it is easier to follow the effects, and discover the causes of them ; research then becomes less painful and tedious, as well as less expensive.

A great deal has been done in this respect, and for the most part in a wrong direction; but as long as artists were the only guides and regulators, the success was very doubtful. As a general rule, the best rectified spirit of wine will not dissolve more than a third of its weight of resinous substances, even when the most soluble are chosen. A boiling heat may cause the spirit to dissolve more, but on the removal of the heat the varnish becomes turbid, and some of the resinous matter is precipitated, or, under the form of a crystallization, lines the interior sides of the vessel.

Some of the formulæ given in the best works still prescribe, in dry matters, a weight equal to two-thirds of that of the solvent. The proportions indicated in the different formulæ given in this work, are more than sufficient for the prescribed quantities of liquid, since there still remains a considerable part which escapes its action. In all cases the process is less embarrassing and more secure from those accidents which are the consequence of a mixture too much charged, and which forms a mass, and is certainly less expensive.

It may here be remarked, that some resins, such as gum sandarac, copal, &c., resist more than others the action of the dissolving fluid. Copal, in particular, exhibits this character. This difficulty, however, may be overcome, with greater or less ease, by diminishing the proportions of these substances. Simple mechanical division, carried as far as possible, and the mixture of a readily soluble substance, such as mastic or frankincense, facilitate solution in a degree which does not take place when the two substances are treated separately, and in the usual manner.

Experience alone can determine in regard to this point. When it is necessary to operate on a considerable mass of matters, the form of the vessel employed is of some importance. Its capacity is not always suited to the quantity it is intended to contain. In this case the first application of the heat tends to agglomerate the resinous ingredients, and thus thwarts the intention of the artist, whose utmost care should be to favor and maintain that state of division which promotes their speedy solution. This object cannot be accomplished by simply stirring, nor even by employing broad-bottomed vessels.

But the consequences of this inconvenience may be greatly diminished by employing some pounded white glass, which has been sifted through a hair-sieve. It must be mixed with the palonized matter before it is united cold with the spirit of wine or of the oil of turpentine; and the division of the parts may still be assisted by stirring it with a rod of white wood, rounded at the extremity.

By this simple mechanism the matter is kept in that state of division necessary for the promptitude and perfection of the solution; and the tumefaction of the liquid, a circumstance much to be dreaded in the process of making varnishes, is prevented. Besides, the weight of the glass, which is greater than that of resins, makes it fall to the bottom of the vessel, where it prevents the adhesion of the softened matters. It is not absolutely necessary that white glass should be used, as green or black bottle glass will answer the purpose. Clean coarse sand, consisting chiefly of silex, is thought by many to be as good as glass. Some have even proposed the use of powdered charcoal. The use of a balneum mariæ is preferable to that of a sand-heat in operations of this kind, because the temperature of the former has a certain fixed point of elevation, which is often exceeded in a sand-heat; and in such a case, there will be great danger of discoloring the varnish, from the application of too great heat.

After the operation, more or less of the resinous substance remains mixed with the glass. This residuum may be reserved for the composition of common varnishes, which are treated over an open fire. Where the matter of the composition does not exceed three pounds, an hour and a half will be, in general, sufficient to complete the solution of the resins, provided that, during this period, the water in the balneum mariæ has been kept in a state of ebullition.

The circular motion with the stick must, however, be still continued for half an hour after the vessel has been removed from the bath. The whole must then be left at rest, to give the undissolved matter time to subside. Next day the clear liquor may be decanted, and put into proper vessels. Some artists strain the varnish while warm, through a piece of linen cloth, and then leave it at rest for a few days to clarify. In both cases, when it is supposed that the solvent is completely saturated with resin, it must be left for some days at rest.

By a high temperature the vehicle becomes charged with a greater quantity of the substances than it can retain when cold. The excess will be precipitated either in whole or in part, according to the season. When the precipitation is pretty extensive, small lumps of resin are formed round the vessel; and sometimes the precipitated resin assumes a peculiar crystallization.

Sometimes the precipitation is not so evident, the varnish remaining a long time turbid, in consequence of the excess of resin continuing in a state of solution, or suspension. When this occurs, add to it a warm solvent, which will dilute the varnish a little; or it may be filtered through cotton.

The operation of filtering through cotton is very simple. Arrange several funnels in as many appropriate receivers, as shown at PLATE I., FIG. 4, and place in the pipe of each funnel a small ball of carded cotton, about one inch in thickness; press this ball towards the point of the cone, to squeeze the cotton together, and place over it a small plate of lead pierced with several holes. Fill the funnels with varnish, and lay over the vessel a glass cover, or a few sheets of paper. The varnish which passes through the cotton is at first not very limpid; but when the cotton has imbibed a sufficient quantity, the liquor passes very clear.

The first portion of filtered varnish is then to be poured again into the funnels; and the filtration being continued, the result will be a very bright varnish. This filtration, which is soon performed, is indispensably necessary for every kind of varnish intended to be applied to delicate articles, such as cut-paper works, valuable furniture, paintings, philosophical instruments, &c. Care must be taken to keep the funnels full, and particularly not to leave the cotton uncovered, else it would become encrusted with a stratum of dry varnish, which would be likely to impede any further filtration. When the whole is filtered, it will be proper to wash all the vessels with spirit of wine, or warm oil of turpentine, according to the nature of the solvent. The product of the washing may be kept in reserve until a new quantity of varnish is made.

Those who prepare varnishes, make other compositions which they intend, in general, for wainscoting, ceilings, common furniture, &c. Some prepare them in open vessels, and in the open air, in consequence of the accidents which sometimes take place when alembics are used. It is much easier to save a matter from inflammation, which is seen to rise, than one enclosed in metallic vessels, where its tumefaction is not observed. This labor on the first view appears to be easy. It requires practice, though, and perseverance to obtain the required result without accident, and to quiet the well-grounded fears which those in the neighborhood may conceive of the danger likely to arise from this process.

It will be right and proper to perform the operation in day-time, and in the middle of a spacious court or garden. The vessel should be furnished with high edges, that the torrent of vapors which escape may not communicate with the undulating flame which often extends beyond the fireplace.

Care must also be taken to dispose the vessel in the furnace in such a manner as to cover the fire entirely, and to prevent any portions of the varnish which may be thrown up by a false movement of the spatula from falling into it. The precautions to be observed are not confined to the manipulations usual on such occasions. When the solution is completed, it is customary to deposit the varnish in an apartment, or work-shop, to cool, and also to give it time to clarify. This apartment then becomes filled with inflammable vapor, to which fire may be communicated by an inflamed body.

These vapors are the more dangerous, as they sometimes extend to a great distance, even beyond the apartment, so that the contact of a lighted taper may occasion an explosion which might ignite the evaporating substance itself. Therefore, great care must be taken not to enter with a candle into an apartment which may contain vapors so highly inflammable. Although the method of making varnish in open vessels has some advantages, it is not free from inconveniences. The artist may carry on his operation in more security: he can easily prevent the tumefaction of the matter, and, consequently, those accidents which result from it.

By means of continued motion, he can also supply the means of escape to the vapors in a state of expansion; and he may renew the surfaces of the resin which touch the bottom of the vessel, and which, by being altered, might discolor the varnish.

This is the favorable side of the method; but the reverse must also be exhibited. This process occasions a very great loss of spirit of wine, or oil of turpentine, in consequence of the vapors which rise from the mass. The vapors, it must be recollected, are the purest part, and contribute most to the excellence of the varnish—to its pliability and lustre. The effect which the constant vapor of the oil of turpentine may produce on the nerves of the artist exposed to it, ought also, if possible, to be avoided.

However great may be the precautions taken in processes of this kind, as they have not always been sufficient to prevent serious accidents, this is sufficient to justify the fears of individuals who reside in the neighborhood of the varnisher, and to excite the vigilance of the city authorities to confine to the outskirts all establishments of this kind. It is, therefore, considered a duty to obviate, or lessen, by improving the form of the vessels and apparatus in the making of varnish, the dangers to which the varnish-maker, as well as tne community, is exposed. To do this to a good advantage, it will be requisite to give here a list of instruments, &c., necessary in the art of the varnish-maker. The premises of the varnish-maker must be accompanied with a court or yard for the preparation of the varnishes, in order that he may be protected, as well as his neighbors, from the damage which may be occasioned by negligence or other causes. Liquid varnishes require to be kept in glass or stone ware. Varnishes should be kept in large, strong black bottles, with a wide mouth, for the convenience of taking them out; but as light has a powerful influence on them, and renders them thick, it is recommended that the bottles be wrapped in sheep's skin or parchment, folding it round the neck, and tying it with several turns of pack-thread.

This addition is attended with the double advantage of guarding against the action of light, and of preventing those accidents which result from percussion. Drying oils are less delicate than varnishes made with spirit of wine or oil of turpentine. They may be preserved exceedingly well in stone-ware jars, in large bottles, or in leaden vessels, with a wide mouth.

Leaden vessels are not liable to those accidents which are most to be apprehended; and if this advantage be not sufficient to cause them to be preferred, they possess another well-known and consistent theory, which is, that they add to the drying quality of the varnish. Varnishes are, however, in the large way, generally kept in earthen bottles, made of what is called stone-ware, or in a large black glass bottle packed with straw in a basket, and usually denominated a carboy. A table, weights, and scales, are all the utensils necessary for the workshop of the varnish-maker. The expense of fitting up a laboratory to furnish articles for common consumption, will be very small. The instruments indispensably necessary are: An alembic, constructed according to the principles explained in this work, with a refrigerator, and portable furnace.

Should the operator not choose to go to the expense of the alembic, and the rest of the apparatus elsewhere spoken of, a succedaneum may, in some degree, be found for them in a sand-bath or sand-heat, and the use of retorts, under suitable precautions. A sand-heat is usually formed, in the large way, of an oblong shape, having bricks and mortar for its walls, plates of iron upon which to lay sand, and around the top a ledge, of about six or eight inches deep, of free-stone, to retain the sand; beneath the plates of iron is a wide flue, at the bottom of which is iron grating, and upon which grating is laid the fire; the fire is, of course, when kindled, enclosed by a door, as in other furnaces, at the end of the sand-heat; the flue communicates with a chimney to carry off the smoke.

The sand is commonly of the depth of six or eight inches; but the quantity and depth of it must depend upon the size of the vessels immersed in it. A retort scarcely needs to be described: it is usually made of green or other glass, and may be made to hold from a pint to eight or more gallons. It has a long, narrow neck, which is so bent that, when the retort is placed with its contents in the sand, it has a gentle inclination, and will conduct whatever liquid is condensed in it into a glass receiver, which is placed on a bench beside the sand-heat; the receiver is luted to the neck of the retort either by a wet bladder-skin, which is the neatest way, or by some other lute. A variety of chemical processes are thus conducted: the vapor raised by the heat being condensed in the neck of the retort, and cooled down in the receiver, (which is usually about the size of the retort) by the large surface which it presents to the air.

But this simple process will not be, in general, adequate to the preparation of spirit varnish; for the vapors rise so soon, and their expansion is so great, that an explosion may often occur. If a glass tube be adapted to the neck of the retort, the receiver removed to a greater distance from the fire, and the tube inserted into it, and if over the tube is placed a vessel of cold water, having a cock at its bottom, which may be made to drop the water gradually on the tube, and thus, by its evaporation, condense the vapors of the spirit within, a succedaneum for the alembic may, in some degree, be found.

This process is generally adopted in the preparation of ether, and for that answers very well. A portable sand-heat may consist of an iron pot, in which the sand is placed, and the pot may be made to suit an ordinary furnace. A few bottles for receivers, that are of a pretty large size, with different funnels of glass and of tin plate. Two or three copper basins of different sizes, according to the extent given to the establishment. Vessels of earthen-ware, to receive the varnish, which is strained through a cloth, and to contain the first deposite. Pieces of board, of the same diameter as the earthen vessels, to serve them as covers. They are more convenient, and not liable to be broken like the earthen-ware ones frequently employed.

Large glass jars, furnished with funnels, filtering the varnishes of the first, second, and third order, as described in the course of this work. A cast-iron pot, polished in the inside, and furnished with a cover, for making varnish of the fifth order. Different spatulas of wood, rounded at the end. A shovel and pair of tongs. Two or three furnaces of different diameters, and, in particular, a small one, with a sand-bath. A small iron-hooped tub, with handles, to contain charcoal.

An iron capsule, or small vessel, with a short handle, to take out the charcoal. Some glass matrasses, of different sizes, for the immediate preparation of alcoholic varnish, which are effected by immersing the matrass in a basin, the water of which is raised to different degrees of heat up to that of ebullition.

A fixed table, some small tables, and a few boxes. A small quantity of white lead paint mixed in linseed oil, for the purpose of applying to burns, which should be rolled out thin and laid on the burnt surface, and then wrapped in cloth, to prevent the more serious consequences of burns that might otherwise follow. An iron mortar, of from twelve to fifteen inches in diameter, with an iron pestle.

Pencils and brushes of different kinds. In regard to those designed for varnish, washing in spirit of wine, or oil of turpentine, as the case may be, will restore them to a clean state. If the varnish has been suffered to dry on or between the hairs of the brush, a few strokes of the hammer or mallet will pulverize and separate the resin, and thus restore the brush to its ordinary softness.

Athough these constitute the chief articles necessary in the work-shop of the varnish-maker, there are others which ingenious artists may find of service, and if so, they should not hesitate to use them.

Of an Alembic, or Still, suitable for the manufacture of Varnish.

The solution of resins cannot be rendered complete, in the common alembic, or still, so that those accidents which arise from the agglomeration of the resins, and particularly from an accumulation of confined vapor, can at the same time be prevented; for the matters becoming tumefied, raise up the capital, and spread with an explosion to the fire, often even to the artist, and in this manner occasion conflagrations.

One of the results from the use of the common alembic, is the discoloration of the varnish, in consequence of an alteration which the resins undergo, by adhering to the bottom of the vessel. These effects would not take place if the construction of the alembic afforded the means of maintaining a circular motion, which would change the points of contact of the enclosed matters; and if, instead of fire being applied immediately, as is the case when a balneum mariæ is employed. These two conditions appear to be answered by the construction of the apparatus described in PLATE II., FIG. 1. It is an alembic and a balneum mariæ with a refrigerator. It consists, first, of a common alembic; second, a balneum mariæ; third, a capital; fourth, another separate piece, which performs the office of a refrigerator, and which is adapted to the alembic at the moment of the operation. The alembic a, FIG. 1, is of copper, and made in the usual form; the aperture, b, terminates in a tube, intended to receive the pipe of a funnel, for the purpose of affording an escape to the vapors which arise from the water in a state of ebullition.

This piece then serves as a receptacle for the water of the balneum mariæ. To this alembic is adapted the balneum mariæ, c, made either of tin or copper: it has the same form as that of the common alembics, and serves to contain the substances which are to compose the varnish. The bottom of it is horizontal, perfectly flat, and about an inch less in diameter than the mouth.

The upper part of this piece is strengthened by a circular band, which serves to cover the joining where the capital is fitted to the alembic. To save expense, this circular band may be made of lead. The diameter of the capital, d, at the base, is proportioned to that of the balneum mariæ, in such a manner as to join with the circular band. This piece terminates in a dome, which at the summit has a pipe or aperture, *e*, half an inch in diameter. A metallic bar, *f*, Fig. 2, soldered at the two extremities, and pierced with a hole corresponding in a vertical direction with the aperture, *e*, and having the same diameter, passes through the middle of the lower end of the capital.

These two apertures are to keep in an exact vertical position a small rod of iron, *g*, connected on the outside with the handle, *h*, which is of wood, and movable. The lower part of this rod, which is continued to the bottom of the balneum mariæ, is furnished with an iron cross, *i*, cut into teeth, while its two extremities are raised up, as seen at *k*: the lower part represents an inverted ⊥, as seen at Fig. 2 and 3. In the upper part of the capital, *d*, is formed a second aperture, *l*, which terminates also in a tube, capable of containing a cock-stopper. This aperture is for the re-introduction of the parts of the liquid obtained by distillation. A conducting tube, *m*, the diameter of which is twice as large as that of the beak of common alembics, taking into account their capacity, proceeds from one of the sides of the alembic.

It is by this canal, which is made of sufficient length, and which is of an equal diameter throughout, that the refrigerator, *n*, is connected with the alembic. The refrigerator, *n*, is constructed in such a manner as to afford a free passage to those matters which might become tumefied, or to condense the vapors which escape from the interior part of the vessel. Both these ends may be accomplished by means of a plain wooden box, well joined together, of an oblong figure, through which a tube, *o*, made of copper, tin, or tin-plate, passes in an oblique direction.

This tube, throughout its whole length, is of the same diameter as that which proceeds from the capital, and is only a continuation of it. When used, the box or trough is filled with cold water. The extremity of this tube terminates in a bent part, *p*, of the same diameter as the rest. Under this part is placed the vessel, *q*, intended to receive the product of the condensed vapors, and, in case of need, the matters which may be raised in the interior part of the apparatus, by the effect of the heat, or in consequence of the consistence which the liquid acquires in this kind of operation, or by the negligence of the artist to stir it during the process. This alembic is placed on a portable furnace of burnt clay, *r*, or on a fixed furnace constructed of bricks, or other materials: it ought not to be too high, lest the artist should be incommoded in managing the handle, *h*.

It has the same form as other furnaces, and is only modified in the manner of placing the chimneys, or vent-holes, which ought to be so disposed as to be sheltered from the contact of the inflammable matters that may fall on the edge of the furnace. This end may be obtained by making the apertures of these chimneys issue through the sides of the furnace, at the distance of two or three inches from the upper edge, and forming over each of them a small projection. The same purpose will be answered by placing on a common furnace a ring, the edge of which, *s*, extends about an inch beyond the exterior diameter of the furnace.

This ring supports the alembic. It may be made out of burnt clay, or of soft stone. Distillation is a process so common that any one may conduct it; but when applied to the present object it requires, on the part of the artist, more attention and care than in ordinary cases. The following, then, is the conduct which should be observed in the preparation of varnish, according to the method here proposed. When the matters are put into the balneum mariæ, cover that part with its capital, and cause the agitator to touch the bottom of it. Lute the two parts exactly, at the place where they are united, with bands of paper and flour paste. Then make a few turns with the handle before heat is applied, to divide the matter; keep the tube, *b*, of the alembic open, and shut closely the tube, *c*. Adapt the refrigerator to the alembic, and cement a few slips of paper over the place where the two vessels are joined; introduce into the alembic such a quantity of water that the body of the balneum mariæ may be half immersed in it, and then kindle the fire. It is of some importance to move the agitator at the moment when the fire is kindled.

If this precaution be neglected, the resinous matter forms itself into a mass, and in that state opposes more resistance to the action of the vehicle. Continue the rotary motion during the whole process, but without too much precipitation. The solution, to be complete, requires only an hour, or an hour and a half, reckoning from the moment when the water begins to boil. If the level of the water employed be fixed at half the interior height of the balneum mariæ, or a little higher, the inconveniences attending too great a quantity of those liquids will be avoided.

By the force of ebullition, part of it is thrown up through the tube, and often incommodes the operation; but there is still a greater inconvenience. When the balneum mariæ is thus completely surrounded by the boiling liquid, the vapor of which has not the means of free escape, the spirit, which becomes hotter as it acquires greater density, in the ratio of its union with the resinous part, tumefies, and escapes as it boils up through the apertures which it meets with; and if it should unfortunately experience the least obstacle to its forced emission, it would burst the vessel, and inundate the artist with matters, which, being soon inflamed by their vapors coming into contact with those that fall into the fire, would expose him to the danger of losing his life in the most excruciating agony, as has often happened.

If the kind of alembic here described were designed for various other uses, like those in chemical laboratories, there might be reason to apprehend the effects of some negligence in regard to the care that ought to be taken to keep tube, b, open, when the distillation is carried on with a balneum mariæ, and to close it with a stopper when distilling with an open fire, that is, without a balneum mariæ. For the present purpose, there is never need of employing this alembic on an open fire; consequently the artist is not under the necessity of shutting the tube, and by these means he avoids those accidents beforehand.

In the contrary case, the vapors of the boiling water being accumulated, and finding no way of escape, would soon burst the apparatus, or would exercise a still greater action on the matters in the bath than if the alembic were filled with boiling water.

In proportion as the heat acts on the substances inclosed in the balneum mariæ, it unites itself to portions of the vehicle, which it reduces to vapor. A part of these vapors are condensed in the inside of the capital, and fall back on the matter. Another part, escaping from the interior of the apparatus, is condensed in the lateral tube, which traverses the refrigerator, and proceeds in a liquid form into the receiver.

This product is composed of the most volatile and most subtile part of the liquid employed for the solution. This loss, if considerable, diminishes the power of the alcohol not volatilized; in a word, the quality of the varnish would suffer by it, if the product of the distillation, when a certain quantity is collected, were not restored to the mass. The aperture, c, is then opened, and a funnel of tin-plate is adapted to it, through which the liquor that has escaped in the form of vapors is returned to the varnish. The cork-stopper is again put in its place; and the circular motion of the agitator is continued.

It is needless to recommend the greatest care that no portion of the liquid introduced may be suffered to fall into the furnace: operators must be aware of the bad consequences. Several compositions require the use of turpentine; but it must not be put into the bath at the same time as the resins, because it would combine with the spirit, and prevent it from exercising the requisite energy on the other substances. The mixture of it must, therefore, be deferred till towards the end of the process. It may be easily added, by first melting it over a slow fire, and introducing it in the same manner as the product of the distillation.

A portion of the same distilled alcohol should be reserved for washing the vessel which contained the turpentine, and the funnel which has been employed. When it is judged that the solution of the resinous matters is finished, the whole of the fire must be removed from the furnace, and the circular motion of the agitator continued for half an hour, leaving some intervals of rest. When the apparatus has in some measure cooled, a sponge dipped in water may be drawn over the pieces of paper which cover the joints, and they are then to be removed as well as the capital, which has been separated from the refrigerator.

The varnish, being then decanted into proper vessels, it may be strained through a piece of dry linen, or filtered through cotton. This operation should be performed in daytime, lest the inflammable vapors which may escape should be set on fire by candles. The person who undertakes this operation, with the precautions pointed out, will always be secure from those accidents which, in this process, are attended with such terrible effects. It must always be remembered that spirituous varnishes should never be prepared in larger quantities than may be required for immediate use, because they do not long retain those qualities which render them valuable.

They should also be kept in well-stopped vessels, much of the spirit escaping from them quickly when exposed to the air. When too long kept, they become yellow and greasy. In this respect they are very different from oil varnishes, which improve by time.

In regard to the heat imparted by steam, in the preparation of varnish, it is necessary that the operator should exercise the greatest caution, otherwise much damage may be done; and on no occasion let it be attempted by any except those who fully understand their business.

Most of the resins, when pure, may be mixed by a careful application of heat with spirit of wine, in various proportions. Thus shellac may be mixed with rectified spirit of wine, so as even to retain a considerable degree of hardness, in addition to its tenacity, and forming the best sealing-wax, with, of course, vermilion, and a certain quantity of camphor—the camphor being added in order to make the wax burn well, on which its quality as sealing-wax, in addition to its tenacity and color, depends. So also, if a spirit varnish happen to be exposed to the air, it soon becomes a thick balsam, and only requires the addition of spirit of wine to give it the ordinary limpidity. It is, therefore, evident, that red spirit varnish may be made with the same ingredients which constitute red sealing-wax, by varying the proportions of the spirit of wine. As this red varnish may interest some persons, an excellent formulæ for red sealing-wax is here given, and when it is wanted to be employed as varnish, nothing more is necessary than to add a larger quantity of rectified spirit of wine.

It must not be forgotten, though, that the specific gravity of the vermilion being much greater than the other ingredients, if the varnish be made thin, the vermilion will necessarily be precipitated, thus injuring the quality of the varnish. The red sealing-wax is made thus: Take of Venice turpentine 2 pounds; camphor, 4 ounces; vermilion, $1\frac{1}{4}$ pound; rectified spirit of wine, 16 ounces. Dissolve the camphor first in the spirit of wine, in a suitable vessel, over a slow fire, taking care that no flame touches the evaporating spirit; then add the shellac; and when that has become of a uniform smoothness, by a moderate application of heat, add the turpentine, and lastly the vermilion, which should be passed through a hair-sieve over the melted mass, in order that it may not get into clots.

When the whole is well incorporated, it is ready to be formed into sticks of whatever size may be desired. It may be added, that it is usual to weigh out the soft wax into balls, and roll them on a mahogany table into the lengths desired, and then to flatten them by pressure.

They are polished by being held over charcoal-fire in a chaffing-dish, then drawn over a piece of mutton suet, or tallow candle, and rubbed with a piece of soft leather.

Black sealing-wax is made in a similar manner; but, instead of vermilion, lamp-black is employed. Black resin is also often used in about one-third the quantity of the shellac, as follows :

>Rectified spirit of wine, 8 ounces.
>Camphor, ... 1 ounce.
>Shellac, ... 2½ pounds.
>Black resin, ... 1½ pounds.
>Lamp-black, ... 4 ounces.

Dissolve the camphor in the rectified spirit of wine, then add the shellac, to which pour the resin previously melted, and mixed with the oil of turpentine, using, of course, a moderate heat, and taking care that no flame touches the melting matters.

Such forms may be varied to almost any extent; and it is also obvious that a black and very useful varnish may be made by adding at pleasure either spirit of wine or oil of turpentine, as may suit the taste or interest of the varnisher. But if lamp-black be employed in such forms for varnish, it will be desirable to burn it before it is mixed with the ingredients for a black varnish. It may be useful, too, to observe here, that the Venice turpentine, when employed as above for red varnish, should not contain a fixed oil, unless it has been previously made drying by some of the processes described in another part of this work.

The following formulæ are almost, if not quite, equal to any foreign Venice turpentine which may possibly be obtained, and are well calculated for mixing with most of the formulæ described in the course of this work, and are well worthy the consideration of the artist:

Take of Frankincense, ... 3½ pounds.
Oil of turpentine, . . . 2½ pints.

Melt first the frankincense over a moderate fire, then add gradually the oil of turpentine, and strain the whole through a hair-sieve; or,

Take of Black resin, ... 8 ounces.
Oil of turpentine, . . . 8 ounces.

Melt first the resin, and add carefully afterwards the oil of turpentine; or,

Take of Linseed oil, ... 1 pint.
Frankincense, ... 3½ pounds.
Oil of turpentine, . . . 1½ pint.

Melt and mix as before, taking care that the oil of turpentine and linseed oil have been previously mixed. In this last form, the varnish-maker should be careful to employ a linseed oil which has been previously rendered drying. A few general observations may be made in regard to "turpentine varnishes." When such a varnish is wanted, without any regard to its tenaciousness when dry, the first preparation, as Venice turpentine above, becomes a very good varnish: if it should prove rather too thick, it may be readily made thinner by the addition of oil of turpentine. But if a varnish of a light color be wanted, united also with some tenacity, the last preparation for Venice turpentine will be found the best. The forms for turpentine varnish may be multiplied without end; but from what has been said, the artist will know how to vary them to suit his in erest, his taste, and the permanence of his workmanship.

French Polish, is made in the following manner:

Take of Seed-lac, ...	6 ounces.
Gum juniper, ...	1½ ounce.
Rectified spirit of wine,	32 ounces.
Gum mastic, ...	1 ounce.

All the ingredients should be first reduced to a coarse powder, and then mixed with the rectified spirit of wine, in a vessel which will contain double the quantity, in order that, on being exposed to the moderate heat of a sand-bath, or other moderate heat, room may be given for the expansion of the spirit without bursting the vessel. The mixture should be well shaken, at least once a day, taking care at the same time to loosen the cork during the shaking; a few days will be sufficient to dissolve the resins.

The application of this polish is too well-known to every one conversant with furniture, and therefore need not be here described. Some persons order equal quantities of shellac and seed-lac; but for this variation there can be no necessity; indeed, where brightness of color is wanted, the seed-lac is undoubtedly to be preferred; but when seed-lac cannot be had, shellac may be employed.

Two methods of freeing lac-varnish from the reddish brown color which is natural to it, are resorted to. One consists in dissolving the lac in rectified spirit of wine, and then destroying the color by repeated and careful additions of chlorine in vapor, and of chloride of potash. The other method is to add to a solution of lac in rectified spirit of wine, animal charcoal, by which the same result is obtained.

Balsam of capivi, or copaiva, has been used as a simple varnish : it answers the purpose very well, but is not, perhaps, better than good turpentine.

Artificial Asphaltum.—Coal tar, by gentle evaporation, assumes the appearance of mineral pitch, and at last, by a combination of the process, attains the consistence of asphaltum. This artificial asphaltum is found to answer nearly all the purposes of the natural production in the coarse black varnishes, such as are used for coach-tops, various japanned wares, and other common articles which require protection from rust. The artificial asphaltum has a feature so nearly resembling the natural, that it is difficult to distinguish them by external inspection : the artificial is blacker than the real asphaltum. The most certain method of detecting the difference between them, is by the smell. Artificial asphaltum must be rejected for etching ground, as it contains ammonia, which will be affected by nitric acid.

It appears, also, that genuine Syrian asphaltum is the proper substance for etching ground ; or Burgundy pitch, for such purpose, is scarcely less important.

Black Varnishes of Silhet.—At Silhet, in Bengal, a black varnish is employed of singular lustre and durability. It is obtained from the expressed juice of the marking-nut, *semecarpus anacordium*, and that of the *holigorna longifolia.* Both these nuts contain, in their integuments, numerous cells, filled with a black resinous juice, which is found also in the wood of the tree. It is used as an indelible ink to mark cotton cloth; the color is fixed with quick-lime. The artisans of Silhet combine the juice obtained from both these nuts for a varnish: it is soluble in alcohol, but not in water.

Varnish of Caoutchouc.—Melt the caoutchouc in a close vessel, that it may not inflame; it will require nearly the temperature to melt lead; it must be stirred with a horizontal agitator, rising through the vessel, to prevent burning.

Oil of turpentine should be carefully added to it, which will render it easily applicable, and leaves the substance, when dry, a firm varnish, imperviable to water or moisture of any kind. This is an excellent varnish for preserving iron and steel from rust. The varnish may at any time be removed by a soft brush dipped in warm oil of turpentine.—*Journal of Science.*

Varnish for Balloons.—A solution of caoutchouc in five times its weight of oil of turpentine; and this solution, mixed with eight times its weight of drying linseed oil, by boiling, forms the varnish usually applied to air-balloons.

Caoutchouc Varnish, with Naphtha.—Digest one ounce of caoutchouc, cut into small pieces, in thirty-two ounces of naphtha. When it is dissolved, strain the varnish through a linen cloth. Naphtha is a native, pungent, oily, odoriferous liquid, either colorless or of a pale brown tint, found in springs on the shores of the Caspian Sea, in Sicily and Italy, and also near the town of Raynagoony in the Burman Empire in Asia. The formulæ given above makes a good common varnish, but is not better than oil of tar.

Brunswick Black.—Take of

Asphaltum, ...	2 pounds.
Oil of turpentine, ...	2 pints.
Boiled linseed oil, ...	½ pound.

Melt first the asphaltum, to which add the linseed oil, and afterwards the oil of turpentine.

This varnish is used for grates, and other common purposes; it is best applied warm, or even hot.

Black Japan Varnish.—Take of

Asphaltum, ...	3 ounces.
Boiled linseed oil, ...	4 pints.
Burnt amber, (in powder) . . .	4 ounces.

Oil of turpentine, a sufficient quantity to make the varnish of a proper consistence. Melt first the asphaltum, to which add the linseed oil gradually, it being first made hot; next add the burnt amber, and lastly the oil of turpentine. A useful varnish for leather.

White hard Varnish.—Take of

Rectified spirits of wine, ...	8 pints.
Gum anime, ...	4 ounces.
Gum sandarac, ...	3 pounds.

Let the gums be finely powdered, and then added to the spirit of wine, a little at a time, stirring the mixture.

Put it into a two-gallon can, in a warm place, stirring the mixture till the gums are dissolved, when it may be strained, and is fit for use.—*Whitlock.*

Sheldrake's Copal Varnish.—Take of copal, broken in small pieces, ... 2 ounces.
    Spirits of ammonia, ... 2 ounces; or,
    Camphor, ... 2 drachms.
    Rectified oil of turpentine, . . . 1 pint.

Stop the vessel with a cock cut in grooves, to admit a portion of the heated vapors to escape; bring it to boil over a brisk fire, so that the bubbles may be counted as they rise; keep the mixture at the same heat; for if the least irregularity, or overheating, takes place, it is useless to proceed. When the solution is complete, let the vessel cool before it is opened. The manufacture of copal varnish, as given by this gentleman, is attended with some inconvenience, and another process is here given. This is made by simply pouring upon copal, reduced to a fine mass in a mortar, colorless oil of turpentine to about one-third higher than the copal, and triturating the mixture occasionally in the course of the day; the next morning it may be poured off for use. Successive portions of oil of turpentine may be mixed with the copal, and will become charged with it as a varnish.

Shellac Varnish.—Take of the best shellac, finely powdered, ... 5 ounces.
    Rectified spirit of wine, ... 2 pints.

The mixture should be placed in a gentle heat, till the shellac is dissolved.

The reader's attention is again called to the necessity of employing the greatest caution in the preparation of varnish of almost every kind; and especially of those which contain ingredients that are readily converted into vapor by the application of heat.

DIVISION OF VARNISHES INTO FIVE CLASSES, WITH INSTRUCTIONS FOR PREPARING THEM, &c.

CLASS THE FIRST.

Varnishes, possessing a drying quality, made with Rectified Spirit of Wine.

No 1.—Take of Gum mastic, . . . 6 ounces.
   Spirit of wine, ... 32 "
   Gum sandarac, ... 3 "
   Glass, coarsely powdered, . 4 "
   Very clear Venice turpentine, 3 "

Reduce the mastic and sandarac to fine powder; mix this powder with white glass, from which the finest parts have been separated by means of a hair-sieve; put all the ingredients with the spirit into a short-necked matrass, and adapt it to a stick of white wood, round at the end, and of a length proportioned to the height of matrass, that it may be put in motion. Expose the matrass in a vessel filled with water, made at first a little warm, and which must afterwards be maintained in a state of ebullition for one or two hours.

The matrass may be made fast to a ring of straw. The first application of the heat tends to unite the resins into a mass: this union is opposed by keeping the matters in a state of rotary motion, which is easily effected by means of the stick, without moving the matrass. When the solution is complete, add to it the turpentine; after which the matrass must be left in the water for half an hour, when it must be taken out, and the varnish continually stirred till it is somewhat cool. Next day it is to be drawn off and filtered through cotton. By these means, it will become exceedingly limpid. The glass directed to be used is merely to divide the ingredients of the mixture, and thus facilitates the solution of the resins in the spirit; besides which, as its weight exceeds that of resins, it prevents them from adhering to the bottom of the matrass; it also prevents the discoloration of the varnish when a sand-bath is employed, as is commonly the case.

No. 2.—Take of pounded copal, of an amber color, once liquified, according to the method hereafter to be described, ... 3 ounces.

Clear turpentine, ... $2\frac{1}{2}$ "
Powdered glass, ... 4 "
Gum sandarac, ... 6 "
Gum mastic, ... 3 "
Rectified spirit of wine, . . . 32 "

These ingredients are to be mixed, and pursue the same plan as directed in No. 1. This varnish is designed for articles subject to friction, such as furniture, chairs, fan-sticks, mouldings, &c., and even metals, to which it may be applied with success. There is great durability given to it by the sandarac.

No. 3.—Take of Gum mastic, . . . 2 ounces.
    Gum sandarac, ... 8 "
    Clear turpentine, ... 2 "
    Rectified spirit of wine, . . 32 "
    Pounded glass, ... 4 "

Used as the preceding, for the same articles.

In order to avoid repetition, it may not be amiss to state here, that all gums or other hard bodies which can be pulverized, should invariably be reduced to a state of gross powder, before being submitted to the action of any solvent. If the bodies be tough, or very adhesive, such as is sometimes the case with gum elemi, they should be divided by cutting into small pieces, in order that the spirit or other menstruum may more readily act upon them.

Class Second.

Varnishes which, though Spirituous, are less drying than Class the First.

Nos. 4 and 5 are for cut-paper works, dressing boxes, &c.

No. 4.—Take of Gum elemi, . . . 4 ounces.
    Gum sandarac, ... 6 "
    Camphor, ... $\frac{1}{2}$ ounce.
    Gum anime, ... 1 "
    Pounded glass, ... 4 ounces.
    Rectified spirit of wine, . 32 "

Make the varnish according to the method already directed. The soft resins may be pounded with the dry bodies. The camphor is to be added in pieces. These varnishes of the second class admit of modifications in the nature of the substances which concur towards their formation. They are not so dry as those of the first class. They give pliability, brilliancy, and solidity to the compositions, without injuring their drying qualities.

No. 5.—Take of Gum anime, ⎫
    Gum elemi,   ⎬ of each, 2 ounces.
   Frankincense, ... 6 "
   Rectified spirit of wine, . . 32 "

Make the varnish with the precautions directed for No. 1. Varnishes composed according to the last two formulæ, may be employed for the same purposes as those which form the first class. They are much fitter, though, for ceilings and wainscoting, colored or not colored: they may even be employed as a covering to parts painted with strong water colors.

No. 6.—Take of Shellac, ... 2 ounces.
    Gum sandarac, ... 6 "
    Rectified spirit of wine, . . . 32 "
    Yellow rosin, ⎫
    White glass, pounded, ⎬ of each, 4 "
    Clear turpentine, ⎭

The varnish to be made according to the directions given for No. 1. This varnish is suited for wainscoting, small articles of furniture, balustrades, and railings in the inside of a house.

No. 7.—Take of Seed-lac, ... 2 ounces.
Gum sandarac, ... 4 "
Pounded glass, ... 4 "
Gum mastic,
Gum Benjamin, } of each, . . 1 ounce.
Venice turpentine, ... 2 ounces.
Rectified spirit of wine, . . . 32 "

The gum sandarac and lac render this varnish durable; t may be colored with a little saffron or dragon's blood. This being slightly colored, is suitable for violins and other stringed instruments, and even for furniture of plum-tree wood, mahogany, and rose-wood.

No. 8.—Take of Venice turpentine, . . 2 ounces.
Gum sandarac, ... 2 "
Seed-lac, ... 5 "
Gum elemi, ... 1½ ounce.
Rectified spirit of wine, . . 24 ounces.
Pounded glass, ... 5 "

This varnish is suitable for boxes or furniture made of box-wood, root of trees, &c.

No. 9.—Take of amber or copal, ground
fine, ... 2 ounces.
Seed-lac, ... 6 "
Hay saffron, ... 36 grains.
Dragon's blood, ... 40 "

Extract of red saunder's wood,
obtained by water, . . . 30 grains.
Rectified spirit of wine, . . . 40 ounces.
Pounded glass, ... 4 "

To apply this varnish to articles of ornaments of brass, expose them to a gentle heat, and dip them into the varnish. Two or three coatings may be applied in this manner if necessary. The varnish is durable, and has a beautiful color. Articles varnished in this manner may be cleaned with water or a piece of dry rag. This varnish gives a gold tint to all articles of brass.

No. 10.—Take of Gum sandarac, } of each, 2 ounces.
Gum elemi,
Gamboge, ... $\frac{3}{4}$ ounce.
Turmeric root, ... $\frac{3}{4}$ "
Dragon's blood, ... 1 "
Seed-lac, ... 1 "
Hay saffron, ... 12 gains.
Rectified spirit of wine, . . . 20 ounces.
Pounded glass, ... 3 "

A tincture of saffron and of the turmeric root must first be made by infusing them together in the spirit of wine for twenty-four hours, in a moderately warm place. The tincture must be strained through a piece of clean linen cloth, and the residuum ought to be strongly squeezed. This tincture is to be poured over the dragon's blood, the gum elemi, the seed-lac, and the gamboge, all pounded and mixed with the glass. The varnish is then to be made according to directions already given.

It may be applied with great advantage to philosophical instruments. The use of it might also be extended to various cast or moulded articles with which furniture is ornamented. If the dragon's blood impart too high a color, the proportion may be lessened at pleasure, as well as that of the other coloring matters.

No. 11.—Take of amber, } of each, . 2 ounces.
Gamboge,
Dragon's blood, ... 60 grains.
Seed-lac, ... 6 ounces.
Extract of red saunder's wood
    in water, ... 24 grains.
Rectified spirit of wine, . . 36 ounces.
Pounded glass, ... 4 "
Hay saffron, ... 36 grains.

Grind the amber, the seed-lac, gamboge, and dragon's blood, together; then mix them with the pounded glass, and add the spirit, after having previously formed with it an infusion of the saffron and of the extract of saunder's wood.

The varnish must then be completed as before. The metal articles intended to be covered by this varnish are heated, and those which will admit of it, are immersed in packets. The tint of the varnish may be varied by modifying the proportions of the coloring substances. The use of spirituous varnishes will long be preferred to that of the varnishes which are to form the third and fourth class; which, however, are far superior in all cases where it is necessary to add durability to the other qualities required. The varnishes of these two first classes bear polishing as well as the hardest compositions which constitute the three other classes; but as they are more delicate, they require modifications in the operation. It is never begun with pumice stone. Most of these varnishes are designed for covering preliminary preparations, which have a certain degree of lustre.

They consist of cement, colored or not colored, covered with landscapes and figures cut out in paper, which produce an effect under the transparent varnish. Most of the dressing-boxes, and other small articles of the same kind, are covered with this particular composition, which, in general, consists of three or four coatings of Spanish white, pounded in water, and mixed up with common glue.

The first coating is smoothed with pumice stone, and then polished with a piece of new linen and water. The coating in this state is fit to receive the intended color, after it has been ground with water and mixed with glue diluted with water. The cut figures with which it is to be embellished are then applied, and a coating of gum or isinglass is spread over them, to prevent the varnish from penetrating the preparation, and from spoiling the figures. The operation is finished by applying three or four coatings of varnish, which, when dry, are polished with tripoli and water, by means of a piece of cloth. A lustre is then given to the surface with starch and a bit of soft cloth of any kind.

Class Third.

This class of varnishes are less exposed to the alterations to which those of the two preceding classes are sometimes subject. The nature of the solvent is here different: oil of turpentine is here substituted in the place of spirit of wine. Almost all the resinous substances, and even the coloring substances hitherto employed, are used in this third class, and by their various mixtures with the oil, concur to accomplish the same views, and produce the same results. It must not be supposed, though, notwithstanding what has been here said, that the properties of spirit of wine, and those of oil of turpentine, are identical; they differ in many respects.

Spirit becomes changed with some particular substances which are not soluble in the oil: of this kind are certain coloring matters, such as indigo, turnsole, red saunders-wood, saffron, &c. On these oil of turpentine produces no effect. In like manner, also, oil of turpentine, under certain circumstances, exerts all the energy of solution on copal, which resists spirit unless it be divided by a soluble body.

At any rate, what it would dissolve without an intermediate substance, would not be sufficient to constitute a varnish. Varnishes made with oil are superior to those composed with spirit. The former unite pliableness and smoothness to brilliancy and durability: they yield better to the operation of polishing, and are less liable to crack than spirituous varnishes. All these qualities, which are well-known, ought to induce artists to prefer this class in all cases where the preservation of the articles to which they are applied, is an object of importance.

This preference is necessary in particular for valuable paintings. In spirituous varnishes the deposit of resinous matter, divided and in a state of complete solution, is sooner formed, according as the season, or circumstances arising from an artificial temperature, accelerate the evaporation of the dividing fluid. The nature of this fluid is sufficiently known; and it gives no reason to suspect that any of its parts incorporate with the resinous molecules, the precipitation of which confirms the effect of a varnish: the alcohol then evaporates entirely. The case is not the same with oil of turpentine, nor with other liquids which have all the characters of oils. They are not susceptible of entire evaporation. The less volatile oils are, the greater will be the solidity of the varnishes resulting from their mixture with resins, and *vice versa*. Oil of turpentine, and oils of greater density, which are still better, would alone form varnishes by repeated application.

Spirit of wine in this case, would disappear without leaving any trace. The consistence which varnishes acquire from oil of turpentine, is often increased by that arising from the particular nature of the matters which form part of the changing varnishes, and particularly of that of the varnishes distinguished by the name of mordants.

In giving the formulæ for varnishes of this third class,

the order will be followed as indicating the degree of their tenacity, and of their resistance to desiccation.

No. 12.—Take of pure turpentine, . . 1½ ounce.
    Gum mastic, cleaned and
     washed, ... 12 ounces.
    Camphor, ... ½ ounce.
    Oil of turpentine, ... 36 ounces.
    White glass, pounded, . . 5 "

Make the varnish according to the method indicated for No. 1. of the first class. The camphor must be cut into pieces, and the turpentine added when the solution of the resin is completed. But if the varnish is to be applied to old paintings, or paintings which have been already varnished, the pure turpentine may be omitted, as this is here recommended only in cases of a first application to new paintings, and just freed from white of egg varnish.

The varnish designed for paintings ought to be colorless, if possible, that it may communicate no foreign tint to the tones of the painting: it should unite pliability and smoothness to the most perfect transparency. It must not, though, have too much glazing, as the reflection of the light is injurious to the effect. Spirit of wine renders varnishes too dry for paintings, as they split and crack.

No 13.—Take of Gum mastic, . . 2 ounces.
    Oil of turpentine, . . . 32 "
    Fresh frankincense, . . 4 "
    Venice turpentine, . . . 6 "
    Pounded glass, ... 4 "

When the varnish is made with the precautions already indicated, add of prepared nut-oil two ounces. This varnish is intended for grinding colors.

No. 14.—Take of Venice turpentine, . 2 ounces.
   Frankincense, ... 12 "
   Oil of turpentine, ... 32 "
   White glass, pounded, . . . 5 "

Make the varnish after the frankincense has been pounded with the glass. This varnish is proper to be used in mixing up colors for grounds.

No. 15.—Take of sandarac or mastic,   4 ounces.
   Seed-lac, ... 4 "
   Turmeric root } of each, . 36 grains.
   Gamboge,
   Dragon's blood, ... $\frac{1}{2}$ ounce.
   Oil of turpentine, . . . 32 ounces.
   Pure turpentine, ... 2 "
   Pounded glass, ... 5 "

A tincture is to be made of the coloring substances; and then add the resinous bodies according to the prescription given at No. 1. These kinds of varnishes are called "changing," because when applied to such as brass, or hammered tin, or wooden boxes, and other furniture, they communicate to them a more agreeable color.

Besides, by their contact with the common metals, they acquire a lustre which approaches that of the precious metals, and to which, in consequence of peculiar intrinsic qualities, or certain laws of convention, a much greater value is attached. It is by means of these changing varnishes that artists are able to communicate to their leaves of silver and copper those shining colors observed on foils. This product of industry becomes a source of prosperity to the manufacturers of buttons and works formed with foil; and in the hands of the jeweller contributes with so much success to produce that reflection of the rays of light which doubles the lustre and sparkling quality of precious stones.

It is to varnish of this kind that we are indebted for the manufacture of "gilt leather." As the colors given by different coloring substances require tones suited to the objects for which they are designed, the artist has it in his power to vary them at pleasure. The addition of anotta to the mixture of dragon's blood, saffron, &c., or some changes in the doses of the more coloring bodies, will easily lead to the modifications desired to be made in the colors. There is one very simple method by which artists may be enabled to obtain all the different tints they require:—

Infuse separately 4 ounces of gamboge in 32 ounces of oil of turpentine, and 4 ounces of dragon's blood and an ounce of anotta, also in separate portions of the oil. These infusions may be easily made in the sun. After fifteen days' exposure, pour a certain quantity of these liquors into a flask, and by varying the proportions you will obtain different shades of color. These infusions may be employed also for spirituous changing varnishes; but in this case, the use of saffron, as well as that of red saunder's wood, which does not succeed with oil of turpentine, will give the tone necessary for imitating with other tinctures the color of gold.

The fat golden varnish, already described, acquires its color from a similar mixture of tinctures. This class of less drying varnishes, admits also species which approach nearly to the nature of fat varnishes, and which are known by the name of "mordants."

No. 16.—Take of gamboge, ... $\frac{1}{2}$ ounce.
   Gum sandarac, ... 1 "
   Gum mastic, ... 1 "
   Oil of turpentine, ... 6 ounces.
   Turpentine, ... $\frac{1}{4}$ ounce.

This composition may be made still less drying by substituting an ounce of the oil of lavender, in place of the turpentine. The compositions of mordants admit of modifications, as a general rule, according to the kind of work for which they are designed. The application of them is chiefly confined to gold.

When it is required to fill up a design with gold-leaf, on any ground whatever, the composition which is to serve as the means of union between the metal and the ground, ought to be neither too thick nor too fluid, because both these circumstances are equally injurious to delicacy in the strokes: it will be requisite also that the composition should not dry till the artist has completed his design. Besides, many artists never make use of prepared mordants. They substitute in their stead an extemporaneous mixture, which they alter at pleasure.

Some prepare their mordant with asphaltum and drying oil, diluted with oil of turpentine. They employ it for gilding pale gold, or for bronzing. Other artists imitate the Chinese, and mix with their mordants color proper for assisting the tone which they are desirous of giving to the gold, such as yellow, red, &c.

Others employ merely the fat varnish of the fifth class, No. 21, to which they add a little red lead. Others make use of thick glue, in which they dissolve a little honey. This is what they call "batture." When they are desirous of heightening the color of the gold, they employ this glue, to which this leaf adheres exceedingly well. Here is a good composition for the purpose: its qualities are fit for every kind of application, and more particularly for that of metals:

Take boiled oil and expose it to a strong heat in a pan; when a black smoke is disengaged from it, set it on fire, and extinguish it a few moments after by putting on the cover of the pan. Then pour the matter, still warm, into a heated bottle, and add to it a little oil of turpentine. This mordant dries up very speedily: it has body, and adheres to, and strongly retains, gold-leaf when applied to wood, metals, and other substances. These examples are sufficient to show the nature of the varnishes which compose the third class. The following class will make the reader acquainted with others which have still more solidity. Under the head No. 25, will be found another mordant, still fatter, with which brown colors may be mixed.

Class Fourth.

Varnishes of Copal, made with Ether and Oil of Turpentine.

The dry nature of the resins which form the basis of the three preceding classes of varnishes and their friability, announce that solidity is not one of their inherent qualities. The merit of the most of these compositions seem to be confined to their drying quality and to their brilliancy. The two following classes will unite to these first characters consistence and solidity.

No. 17.—Take of sulphuric ether, . 2 ounces.
Copal, of an amber color, . $\frac{1}{2}$ ounce.

Reduce the copal to very fine powder, and introduce it by small portions into the flask which contains the ether; close the flask with a glass or cork-stopper, and, having shaken the mixture for half an hour, leave it at rest till the next morning. In shaking the flask, if the lids become covered with small undulations, and if the liquor be not exceedingly clear, the solution is incomplete. In this case add a little more ether, and leave the mixture at rest. The varnish is of a light lemon color. It has been applied to wood with complete success, and the glazing it produced united lustre to solidity.

No. 18.—Take of oil of turpentine, . . 8 ounces.
Copal, of an amber color, in powder, ... $1\frac{1}{2}$ ounce.

The oil is to be exposed to a water-bath, in a wide-mouthed matrass with a short neck : as soon as the water of the bath begins to boil, throw into the oil a large pinch of copal powder, and keep the matrass in a state of circular motion. When the powder is incorporated with the oil, add more of it ; and continue in this manner till you observe that there is formed an insoluble deposit.

Then take the matrass from the bath, and leave it at rest for some days ; draw off the clear varnish, and filter it through cotton. At the moment when the first portion of the copal is thrown into the oil, if the powder precipitate itself in lumps, it is needless to proceed farther. This effect arises from two causes : either the oil does not possess the proper degree of concentration or it has not been sufficiently deprived of water. Exposure to the sun, employing the same matrass, to which a cork-stopper should be added, will give it the qualities requisite for the solution of copal. This effect will be seen by the disappearance of the portion of copal already put into it. To obtain this varnish colorless, it may be proper to rectify the oil of the shops, and to give it the necessary density by exposure to the sun in bottles closed with cork-stoppers, leaving an interval of some inches between the stopper and the surface of the liquid.

A few months are thus sufficient to communicate to it the required qualities. This solution of copal in oil of turpentine is an exceedingly durable varnish, and quite brilliant. It resists percussion much better than the enamel of toys, which often becomes scratched and whitened by friction; it is susceptible also of a fine polish. It is applied with the greatest success to philosophical instruments, and the paintings with which vessels and other utensils of metal are decorated.

No. 19.—Take of oil of turpentine, . . 6 ounces.
   Copal, in powder, ... 1 ounce.
   Essential oil of lavender, . 2 ounces.

The oil of lavender is to be put into a matrass of a proper size, placed on a sand-bath, made hot by an Argand's lamp, or over a moderate coal fire. Add to the oil, while very warm, and at several times, the copal powder, and stir the mixture with a stick of white wood rounded at the end. When the copal has entirely disappeared, add at three different times the oil of turpentine, almost in a state of ebullition, and keep continually stirring the mixture.

When the solution is completed, the result will be a varnish of a gold color, very durable and brilliant, but less drying than the preceding.

No. 20.—Take of clear turpentine, . . 1 ounce.
   Copal, ... 4 ounces.

Put the copal, coarsely powdered, into a varnish-pot, and give it the form of a pyramid, which must be covered with turpentine. Shut the vessel closely and, placing it over a gentle fire, increase the heat gradually, that it may not attack the copal.

As soon as the matter is well liquified, pour it upon a plate of copper, and when it has resumed its consistence, reduce it to powder. Put half an ounce of this powder into a matrass with four ounces of rectified oil of turpentine, and stir the mixture till the solid matter is entirely dissolved.

No. 21.—Take of essential oil of lavender, 6 ounces.
    Pulverized copal, ... 2 "
    Camphor, ... $\frac{1}{8}$ ounce.
    Oil of turpentine, a sufficient quantity, according to the consistence required to be given to the varnish.

Put into a phial of thin glass, or into a small matrass, the oil of lavender and the camphor, and bring the oil and the camphor to a slight state of ebullition. Then add the copal powder in small portions, which must be renewed as they dissolve in the liquid. Favor the solution by stirring it with a stick of white wood; and when the copal is incorporated with the oil, add the oil of turpentine boiling, but care must be taken to pour it in at first only in small portions. Camphor, which has long been employed as a medium to facilitate the solution of resin in the composition of varnish destined for valuable paintings, might be applied in this process in doses of from 24 to 30 grains for every ounce of the oil of lavender.

It has the singular property of altering the consistence of the driest resins, and of rendering them soft.

It softens them to such a degree that it is impossible to preserve the consistence of plaster, if the quantity be carried beyond thirty or forty grains for each ounce of resin

Description of a Furnace, intended for the liquifaction of Copal and Amber.

This furnace, a section of which is represented at Fig. 1, Plate I., may be entirely constructed of burnt clay, three large apertures being made in the lower chamber, A, which supplies the place of an ash-hole in the common furnaces. The upper part of these apertures is arched, and the pillars or solid parts between them should be as narrow as possible, in order to enable the artist with facility to extract the liquified matter, and even to mix it with the drying oil, if this kind of varnish be required. The upper part, B, or fire-place of the furnace, is separated from the lower part, A, by a bottom or plate, which answers the same purpose as a grate in common furnaces.

This plate has in the middle a circular aperture, the diameter of which corresponds to that of the tube, C, which it is designed to receive, and which extends a considerable way below it. This plate may either form one piece with the furnace, or may be movable. In the latter case, it is supported by three projections, or by a circular ledge, which projects inward.

In some furnaces this partition is composed of an iron plate covered with a coating of potter's clay an inch in thickness. This precaution is indispensably necessary to prevent the heat from penetrating to the lower division, A. The sides of the fire-place, B, are pierced with holes an inch in diameter, and distant from each other about three inches. These apertures admit air sufficient to maintain the heat at the degree proper for this kind of operation. The following are the proportions of the three parts of this furnace, which has served for experiments, and in which six ounces of copal were liquefied in the space of ten minutes, without altering its color.

	Inches.
Total height of the furnace,	$17\frac{1}{2}$
Height of the lower chamber, A, including the bottom, which was an inch in thickness,	11
Height of the lower chamber, B, or of the fire-place,	$5\frac{1}{4}$
Diameter, taken at the superior edge of the fire-place, B,	$9\frac{1}{2}$
Diameter of the same, taken at the bottom, or partition,	7

This part decreases in diameter $2\frac{1}{2}$ inches, tapering towards the lower part of the furnace, A. The tube, c, is conical at the upper extremity, and cylindrical towards the bottom: it is $9\frac{1}{2}$ inches in length, $4\frac{1}{2}$ in diameter at the top, and $2\frac{1}{2}$ towards the middle. Both ends of it are open.

The tube, c, is placed in the aperture formed in the middle of the partition, in such a manner as to rise three or four inches into the fire-place. The place where it joins to the partition is luted with clay, to prevent the ashes or small coal from falling down. When this arrangement is made, the net, D, (see Fig. 2) made of brass wire, worked very open, is placed in the tube.

It has the shape of a funnel, the upper part of which is made fast to a ring of wire, of the same diameter as the upper part of the tube, c. The decrease in the diameter of the tube, c, conduces to the stability of this net, and the conical form of the latter prevents it from coming into contact with the lateral parts of the tube, which is a matter of great importance to preserve the copal from too great alteration by the heat. The copal is placed on this metallic filter in pieces not larger than a small nut, and the whole is closed up with the iron plate or cover, e, an inch in thickness, taking care to lute the joining with clay, to prevent all communication with the external air.

A shallow dish or capsule, f, filled with water, (Fig. 3) is placed under the bottom of the tube, c, in such a manner that the tube is immersed in the water two or three times. The fire-place, d, being filled with burning coals, so as to rise above the iron cover of the tube, the first action of the heat on the copal is discovered by a kind of crackling, the consequence of its dilation, which makes it split into small pieces; soon after which it melts. A small iron pallet-knife, terminating in an elbow, is introduced under the tube, and moved in such a manner as to cause the liquid part of the copal to fall down into the water, and to bring it under the solid form towards the edge of the capsule.

When the operation is finished, the copal is spread out on dry linen cloths, or on unsized paper, and then dried by a gentle heat. While the melted copal is falling down, a very small portion of oil separates, which remains fluid after the operation. It floats on the water as well as the copal, and gives to the latter a greasy appearance. But when the tube is of sufficient length, there will be no necessity for immersing the end of it in the water, or even for receiving the matter in the water; but in this case, a kind of smoke will escape, which may be offensive to the operator.

The essential point is to regulate the fire in such a manner as not to alter the color of the copal. If a very thick smoke issues through the lower aperture of the tube when red-hot, and when the drops fall into the water rise into bladders and burst, there is reason to conclude that the fire is too great.

No. 22.—Take of oil of turpentine, . 20 ounces.
    Copal, liquefied, ... 3 "

Place the matrass containing the oil in a water-bath, and when the water is warm add the copal in small quantities. Keep stirring the mixture, and add no more copal till the former be incorporated with the oil. If the oil takes up three ounces of it, add a little more; but stop when the liquid becomes cloudy, and leave the varnish at rest. If it be too thick, dilute it with a little warm oil, after having heated it in the balneum mariæ. When cold filter it through cotton. This varnish has a good consistence, and is as free from color as the best spirituous varnish.

When extended in one stratum over smooth wood, which has undergone no preparation, it forms a very brilliant glazing, which, in the course of two days in summer, acquires all the solidity that may be required. Painted boxes, and all small articles, colored or not colored, where it is required to make the veins appear in all the richness of their tones, call for the application of this varnish, which produces the most effect, and which is more durable than turpentine varnishes composed with other resinous substances.

Class Fifth.

Though the varnishes of this class are the most durable, they are slower in drying. They are designed for objects exposed to friction or percussion, and are particularly employed for the decoration of carriages. They are applied to wood, to iron, brass, and also to copper; they are likewise used for waiters, Argand's lamps, teapots, and other utensils of the same kind.

Although the proportions indicated in the different formulæ for this fifth class of varnishes have been proved, the last portions of the copal, and particularly of the amber, must not be melted if the varnish be required as little colored as possible. The portions of the amber which have escaped liquefaction can be easily separated by a sieve, or by deposition.

No. 23.—Take of oil of turpentine, . 16 ounces.
           Picked copal, ... 16 "
           Prepared linseed or poppy
              oil, ... 8 "

Liquefy the copal in a matrass over a fire, and then add the linseed oil, or oil of poppies, previously made very hot; when these matters are incorporated, take the matrass from the fire; stir the matters till the heat has in part subsided, and then add the oil of turpentine, previously made warm. Strain the whole while still hot through a piece of linen, and put the varnish into a wide-mouthed bottle. By keeping it improves, and becomes clearer. In general, there is much advantage in not employing too violent heat.

The varnish by these means succeeds better, and acquires less color. If it afterwards becomes too thick, add a little warm oil of turpentine, that the mixture may take place more speedily.

No. 24.—Take of Venice turpentine, . 1½ ounce.
           Copal, of an amber color, . . 6 ounces.
           Oil of turpentine, ... 6 "
           Prepared linseed oil, . . . 18 "

It is customary to place the Venice turpentine over the copal, reduced to small fragments, in the bottom of an earthen or metal vessel, or in a matrass exposed to such a heat as to liquefy the copal; but it is more advantageous to liquefy the latter alone, to add the linseed oil, previously made very hot, then the Venice turpentine liquefied, and, in the last place, the oil of turpentine. If the varnish be too thick, some oil of turpentine may be added. It is employed in the manufactories for watch-cases, in imitation of tortoise-shell.

No. 25.—Take of Venice turpentine, or
           gum lac, ... 2 ounces.
           Amber, coarsely powdered, 16 "
           Oil of turpentine, . . . 15 "
           Prepared linseed oil, . . . 10 "

The circumstances of the process are the same as those prescribed for the preparation of the copal varnish, No. 21.

No. 26.—Take of drying linseed oil, Oil of turpentine, } each, 10 ounces.
Amber or copal, of 1 infusion, 4 "

Put the whole into a pretty large matrass, and expose it to the heat of a balneum mariæ, or move it over the surface of an uncovered chafing dish, but without flame, and at the distance from it of two or three inches. When the solution is completed, add still a little amber or copal, to saturate the liquid. Then pour the whole on a filler prepared with cotton, and leave it to clarify by rest.

If the varnish is too thick, add a little warm oil of turpentine, to prevent the separation of any of the amber. This varnish is colored, but far less so than those composed by the usual method. When spread over white wood, without any preparation, it forms a solid glazing, and communicates a slight tint to the wood.

No. 27.—Take of gum lac, ... 2 ounces.
  Amber, ... 8 "
  Oil of turpentine, . . . 16 "
  Drying linseed oil, . . . 8 "

Dissolve separately the gum lac; then add the amber, prepared and pulverized, with the linseed oil and turpentine very warm. When the whole has lost a part of its heat, mix in relative proportions tinctures of anotta, of turmeric root, gamboge, and dragon's blood, as mentioned at No. 10. When this varnish is applied to white metals, it gives them a gold color.

No. 28.—Take of Venice turpentine, . 8 ounces.
Boiled linseed oil, ... 16 "
Naples yellow, ... 5 "

Heat the oil with the turpentine, and mix the Naples yellow pulverized. This is a fat varnish, which may serve as a mordant to gold, and at the same time to dark colors. Naples yellow is chiefly an oxide of lead. It is substituted here for resins, on account of its drying quality, and, in particular, of its color, which resembles that of gold. Great use is made of this varnish in applying gold-leaf. The yellow may be omitted when varnish of this kind is to be applied to solid and colored coverings.

In this case, an ounce of litharge, to each pound of composition, may be substituted in its stead, without this mixture doing any injury to the color which is to constitute the ground.

No. 29.—Take of boiled linseed oil, . 16 ounces.
Oil of turpentine, ... 16 "
Caoutchouc, or India rubber, 16 "

Cut the caoutchouc into thin slips, and put them into a matrass, placed in a hot sand-bath. When the matter is liquified, add the linseed oil in a state of ebullition, and then the oil of turpentine, warm. When the varnish has lost a great part of its heat, strain it through a piece of linen, and preserve it in a wide-mouthed bottle.

This varnish dries very slowly—a fault which is owing to the peculiar nature of the caoutchouc.

Gold-colored Varnish for Wood or Metal.—Take two ounces of gum sandarac, one ounce of litharge of gold, four ounces of clarified linseed oil; boil them in a glazed earthen vessel till they appear of a transparent yellow, on a gas cooking-stove.

Gold Varnish for Wood or Metal.—One ounce of litharge of gold, two ounces of gum sandrach, four ounces of clarified linseed oil. Boil them together in a glazed earthen vessel to a transparent yellow; to be used with a soft brush.

Bleached Oil for Colorless Varnish.—Cover the bottom of a four-gallon vessel with white lead, to the depth of about six inches, nearly fill it with raw linseed oil; be careful that the vessel is covered with glass; this is necessary not only to keep the dust and other impurities from it, but that it may admit the light and hot rays of the sun. It must remain exposed to the sun till it gets fat and colorless, and it will be fit for use. French yellow is an excellent substitute for white lead, and is used by many varnish-makers in preference, as it speedily draws the coloring matter out of the oil, and soon renders it suitable for the varnish.

Of the various colored Varnishes, with instruction for preparing them.—Glazing on Metallic or other substances.—Preparation of Foils, &c., &c.

Transparent Green.—Artists are often embarrassed in regard to the choice of coloring matters, when they are desirous of communicating a color to a liquid without injuring its transparency. Some coloring parts are susceptible of being dissolved in spirit of wine and in oily substances, but not in water. Some saline preparations of copper are of this nature, while the oxides of copper resist, for the most part, the action of water, but combine with oily liquors.

Other colors require mordants of an acid or alkaline nature before they combine with water, and are incapable of union with oils. Indigo, litmus, cochineal, saffron, and red sandal wood, prove the truth of this statement. To make the transparent green varnish, heat a quantity of copal varnish, and put into it, small quantities at a time, powdered verdigris, (crystallized) until the liquid possesses the properties desired.

Another green color.—The green carbonate of copper, obtained by precipitating a solution of copper in any acid, by a solution of carbonate of potash, if washed and dried, and then mixed with copal varnish, gives a beautiful green color. It is inferior, though, to the preceding composition.

Another green color by composition.—This green may serve as an illustration of the theory of compound colors. The mixture of two simple colors produces a compound color, the tint of which depends on the respective quantities employed. The varnish colored by turmeric root or gamboge, Nos. 15 and 16, mixed with the following varnish, colored by Prussian blue, is more beautiful, smoother, and extensible than either of the green varnishes just described.

Blue color.—Could indigo be incorporated with copal varnish, and communicate its color to it, persons would not be obliged to prepare this color from a substance which alters its limpidity. Prussian blue serves as the basis of this color. The best Prussian blue of the shops communicates to varnish a very transparent blue color; but it has not that richness of reflection and velvety appearance so agreeable to the eye when the extension of which it is capable without being weakened, has been given to it.

When extended over a metallic plate, there are sometimes grains observed in it, which may be owing to its incomplete division, or to the separation of some earthy matter, which even the best Prussian blue of the shops usually contains. This blue, when in a state of purity, unites so completely with copal varnish that its transparency does not seem to be in the least affected by it.

Superb liquid blue.—Sometimes it is the case that circumstances will occur to require the application of copal varnish to a color which may have been mixed up with a gummy or mucilaginous liquid. These circumstances arise from the accidents which happen to enamel.

Opaque enamels resist the action of a mineral acid; and, in like manner, transparent enamels, applied to gold and silver, may be repaired with colors, having mineral acids for their mordant, attention being paid to their particular affinities. In regard to metals, the texture of which is inferior to that of gold or silver, colors with a mordant can be applied only by means of a gummy juice capable of defending the metallic plate from the action of the mordant.

The composition of the color about to be described, as well as that from indigo, which will be spoken of hereafter, belongs to those which require this preliminary precaution. Put into a small matrass or phial, an ounce of fine Prussian blue, reduced to powder, and pour upon it from an ounce and a half to two ounces of strong muriatic acid. The mixture produces an effervescence, and the Prussian blue soon assumes the consistence of thin paste.

Leave it in this state for twenty-four hours; then dilute it with eight or nine ounces of water, and preserve the color thus diluted in a bottle well stopped. The intensity of this color, which is very dark, may be lessened if necessary by more water. If the whole of this mixture be poured into a pint or more of water, it will still be sufficiently dark for washing prints. This color, charged with its mordant, requires the use of gum water, made with gum tragacanth. Mucilage of gum arabic does not possess sufficient consistence. This color, applied with gum water, and covered when dry with copal varnish, would form very beautiful foil.

Yellow.—Turmeric-root and gamboge give very beautiful yellows, and readily communicate their color to copal varnish made with turpentine. Aloes give a varied and orange tint.

Dark red.—Dragon's blood, digested in warm varnish, gives reds, the intensity of which depends upon the quantity of the coloring resin which combines with varnish. The artist, therefore, has it in his power to vary the tones at pleasure. Though cochineal, in a state of division, gives very little color to oil of turpentine in comparison to that which it communicates to water, carmine may be introduced into the composition of varnish, colored by dragon's blood. The result will be a purple red.

Violet.—A mixture of carminated varnish and dragon's blood, added to that colored by Prussian blue, produces violet. From these examples of the communication of colors to copal varnish, every person habituated to the operations of this art, and every amateur possessed of dexterity may readily prepare any color he desires.

From what has been already said, the reader must be convinced that copal varnish, if carefully applied, is capable of producing great richness, splendor, and solidity, when extended over surfaces which are themselves possessed of splendor, as is the case with metallic substances.

This quality renders it proper for articles subject to percussion or to continued friction, and exposed to humidity. The application of a varnish sufficiently solid to resist these, and sufficiently transparent to preserve and even to increase the original metallic splendor, must add, in a considerable degree, to the value of the articles. When the copal varnish is designed for small articles, as a particular distribution of the colors is not required, it may be applied as well by an amateur as by a professed varnisher.

But if large articles are to be varnished, the application of it requires practice and great care. One of the essential conditions relates to the state of the metallic surface. It must be extremely well polished, and then be heated on an iron plate placed over a chafing-dish, till the hand can scarcely bear to touch it; and the heat must be equal in every part of it. When this is done, dip a large flat brush, made of very soft hair, in the varnish, and draw it gently over the whole surface. This operation requires dexterity, that the different strokes of the brush may not be observed. It will, therefore, be proper not to load the brush with too much varnish at once. If these precautions are neglected, the surface of the metal will exhibit undulations, and very often it will be spotted.

Turned articles, if varnished while in the lathe, by means of heat, will always be attended with the greatest success, because the extension of the varnish is more uniform, and the operation facilitates the polishing. When undulations are observed, this defect may be, in part, remedied by bringing the article near the iron plate without actual contact. A gentle heat renders the varnish more uniform. If a gold color be required, two or three successive coatings of colored and changing varnish may be applied, and these must be covered by another coat of the uncolored copal varnish, No. 18.

The coloring parts of the changing varnish of the third class, No. 15, may be also communicated to the copal varnish, or the varnish No. 22, made with copal of one infusion, may be employed. If particular circumstances, determined by the nature of the article intended to be varnished, prevent its being heated, the varnish must be applied cold; but the article may be brought near to the fire or exposed in a stove, the heat of which disposes the varnish to extend itself in a more uniform manner, and to appear with its whole lustre.

A bright sun and pure air produce the same effect.

If these kinds of varnish become stained by use, the article must be washed with warm water, and wiped with a piece of linen rag. The contact of hard bodies is hurtful to them. If the case require it, a little soap may be added to the warm water.

Observations on the application of Copal Varnish for repairing Opaque Enamel.

The properties possessed by these varnishes, which render them proper for supplying the vitreous and transparent coating of enamel, with a coloring equally brilliant, but more solid, and which adheres to vitreous compositions and to metallic surfaces, admit of their being applied to other purposes. By slight modifications they may be used also for repairing opaque enamel which has been broken. These kinds of enamel may be repaired either by colored cements or by colored copal varnish, applied superficially.

On this account they are attended with less difficulty in repairing than transparent enamel, because they do not require the same reflection of light. The intention of the artist will be answered by compositions of paste, the different grounds of which harmonize with the colors or ground of the piece to be repaired, and which may be strengthened by the same tint introduced into the solid varnish with which the articles are glazed. The base of the cement should be pure white, dry clay. If solidity be required, white lead is the only substance that can be substituted for it.

Drying oil of poppy will form an excellent vehicle, and the consistence of the cement ought to be such that it can be easily extended by a knife or spatula, of a moderate degree of flexibility. This sort of paste soon dries. It has the advantage also of forming a ground which contributes to the solidity of the colors applied to it with a brush. The varnish, No. 1, of the first class, is very drying. The application of it will be proper in cases when the speedy repair of the damaged articles is required. In more urgent cases, the paste may be composed of white lead and the copal varnish No. 18, which dries more speedily than oil of poppy; and the colors may then be glazed with the etherous copal varnish of the fourth class, No. 17. The application of the paste will be necessary only in cases when the accident which has happened to the enamel leaves too great vacuity to be filled up by several coats of colored varnish.

But in all cases, the varnish ought to be well dried, that it may acquire its full lustre by polishing. Though it may be more convenient to apply the paste, and then to color it superficially by coats of the requisite colors, cases may occur in which a preference ought to be given to colored cements; and, though any artist may easily determine the kind of matter proper for the purpose, it will no doubt be of some utility to give a short view of the coloring substances recommended by the experience of the best artists.

White.—Spanish white, white lead, white clay. Such of these substances as are preferred ought to be carefully dried. White lead and clays obstinately retain a great deal of humidity, which prevents their adhesion to drying oil or to varnish. The cement then crumbles under the fingers, and does not acquire a body.

Black.—Lamp black, black made of burnt vine-twigs, black of peach-stones. The lamp black must be carefully washed, and afterwards dried. Washing carries off a great many of its impurities.

Yellow.—Patent and Naples yellows, reduced to impalpable powder. These yellows are damaged by the contact of iron and steel: in mixing them up, therefore, an ivory spatula and glass mortar and pestle must be employed. Dutch yellow ochre, or gamboge, according to the nature and tone of the color to be imitated

Blue.—Indigo, Prussian blue, blue verditer, and ultramarine. All these substances must be finely powdered.

Green.—Verdigris, crystallized or distilled verdigris. Compound green, a mixture of yellow and blue. The first two require a mixture of white in proper proportions, from a fourth to two-thirds, according to the tint intended to be given. The white used for this purpose is white lead, or Spanish white, which is less solid.

Red.—Vermilion, red lead, different red ochres, or Prussian reds, &c.

Purple.—Cochineal, carmine, and carminated lakes, with white lead and boiled oil.

Brick red.—Dragon's blood.

Buff color.—Dragon's blood, with a paste composed of flowers of zinc, or, what is still better, a little vermilion.

Violet.—Vermilion mixed with washed and very dry lamp black, or with the black of burnt vine-twigs; and, to render it mellower, a proper mixture of red, blue, and white.

Pearl gray.—White and black, white and blue. For example, white lead and lamp black, white lead and indigo.

It is well known that these mixtures cannot be subjected to fixed rules, in regard to the quantity of the matters which enter into their composition. They must depend on the taste of the artist, and the shade which he is desirous of giving to the color.

All these different methods resemble a lucrative kind of painting, which gives employment to a number of hands; namely, the preparation of FOILS, or colored *laminæ*, used with so much success in the manufacturing of buttons in embroidery, and for ornamenting a variety of toys, of which there is a very extensive and daily consumption. These very thin laminæ of silver, copper, brass, or tin, perform the same office, under the name of foil, and may be distinguished by the name of "false enamel," as enamel covered with colored or uncolored copal varnish.

If the latter seem to differ from foil, by their consistence which depends upon the thickness of the metallic laminæ, and the repeated application of coats of varnish; if they differ also in the nature of the varnish itself, the use of which does not include the "sauces," (by this term is meant the composition employed in making foil) that constitute the coloring part of foil, they certainly seem to have some resemblance in the nature of their composition. To gratify those who may desire to unite the preparation of foils to that of varnishes, all the information which could be obtained on the subject, is here given.

Preparation of Foil.

It will be remembered by the reader, that some coloring substances, of an extracto-gummy nature, dissolve more readily in water than in spirit of wine or essential oils; that other colors, those prepared from mineral substances, as Prussian blue, &c., are only minutely divided without being dissolved. When the nature of the coloring parts which ornament different kinds of foil is examined, it does not always appear to be owing to colored varnishes. Some of these coloring parts belong to that kind of compositions called "sauce," covered afterwards with a transparent varnish which preserves them from the influence of moisture, and which produces with the metallic splendor that beautiful effect with which they are generally attended.

The processes may be varied, with regard to the tone and shades of the colors, which may be easily rendered stronger or weaker. Those which are described below have produced, to a great extent, the desired effect.

Preparation the first.—Immerse isinglass in pure spring water for twenty-four hours, and boil it to complete solution. Strain the whole through a double piece of linen, or a piece of flannel, and evaporate till a trembling jelly is formed.

Preparation the second.—Dip the polished metallic leaves of copper, brass, or tin, (the latter are only employed for gilt leather and for decorating papier mache) which you wish to color, in water mixed with a little aquafortis; for example, an eighth, a tenth, or a twelfth part of acid. This immersion renders the surface of the metal rough. Then wipe it carefully immediately, and, having applied the isinglass, suffer it to dry, that it may receive the color.

Blue color.—The beautiful liquid glue, the composition of which has been given, may be employed for this purpose. Leaves of silver or copper ought to be preferred to those of brass, when colors with a mordant are applied. Any degree of dilution may be given to this blue by the addition of common water.

Another blue.—Take one part of indigo and put it into a phial placed in hot sand, with two parts of sulphuric acid. When the effervescence which takes place has subsided, add ten or twelve parts of pure water. This kind of solution renders the blue very beautiful. The observations made in treating of the preceding blue, in regard to the nature of metallic laminæ, may be applied to this kind of color. They ought to be copper or silver.

Green.—A compound green may be made by mixing a decoction of yellow berries with a little blue liquor. It may be prepared also by the immediate employment of a solution of distilled verdigris, such as that described under this head. The sea-green may likewise be imitated.

Red.—A dark red may be extracted from a decoction of cochineal, the tint of which can be varied by means of a large proportion of water. This red rather inclines to purple. The red of saunder's wood may be extracted by spirit of wine the evaporation of which will furnish the means of concentrating the coloring part. The coloring principle may be extracted also by water, which must afterwards be evaporated, and the extract in them mixed with spirit of wine. A process nearly similar may be employed to apply the rose color of bastard saffron to foil. This coloring part is soluble in carbonate of soda. It is precipitated from the soda by means of the acid of lemon juice, which combines with the alkali. For the present operation, this coloring part is separated from the supernatant water by means of some slips of cotton cloth, or cotton wicks, one end of which is immersed in the liquid, while the other hangs over the edge of the vessel.

All the water is thus drawn off as if through a filter. The coloring part is then mixed with rectified spirit of wine, and spread over the metallic surfaces in successive layers.

Violet.—The coloring part of litmus dissolves readily in water, and produces a coarse violet. It may be brightened by using rectified spirit of wine, which dissolves it as well as water. The coloring part of litmus is held in solution by liquor ammonia. The coloring part which has dissolved in water, in the case of an aqueous decoction, is precipitated by the addition of a little acid of lemon : it then subsides to the bottom of the vessel.

To separate the supernatant water, the same kind of filtration as that used for the decoction of bastard saffron, may be employed. Concentrated decoction of litmus, applied to metallic laminæ, furnishes a speedy method of coloring.

Lilac.—Tie up the litmus in a cloth, and immerse it in water till it gives only a rose color. Then boil it in more water, in which the remaining color will be concentrated, and apply this decoction cold to the metallic laminæ, prepared with a solution of fish-glue.

Ruby color.—Boil carmine, or carminated lake, in water, and when the decoction rises, add a few drops of the liquor of ammonia. Suffer the decoction to form a deposit when cold, and employ it without filtration. A decoction of cochineal might be substituted for the carmine or the lake.

Rose color.—To make rose color, add to the preceding a fresh quantity of water, until it is brought to the required tone. Bastard saffron gives different shades of rose color. A decoction of Brazil-wood, mixed with a solution of tin in aqua regia, gives also tones of rose color.

Poppy red.—Spread a stratum of the ruby color, and over it another of infusion of saffron, prepared by moderation in cold water for forty-eight hours.

Capuchin color, yellow, and jonquil, may be made in this manner by varying the intensity of color.

Plum color, and other browns.—A stratum of lilac color, and over it a stratum of green or blue.

The second and third coats of colors ought not to be applied till the preceding is perfectly dry. Care must be taken also not to pass several times over the same place, because the new color, though cold, loosens the former. It is, therefore, always advantageous to give to the color a very dark tint, because it saves the trouble of going too often over the same surface. These different tints of colors would not have the durability of foil, and would be easily effaced by moisture, were they not preserved by being covered with varnish.

The varnishes generally appropriated to articles of this kind, are those which compose the first class; that is, drying varnishes made with spirit of wine. Nos. 1, 2, and 3, therefore, may be employed in such cases; and, for the better preservation of the copal varnish, No. 18 or No. 22, of the fourth class, may be used. At first it will emit some smell, but this may be remedied by a coating of spirituous varnish. Articles of this kind do not require much durability in the varnish.

Of the process for preparing Waxed or Varnished Cloth, Varnished Silk, Court Plaster, various methods of Staining Wood, &c.

Common Wax-Cloth, or Varnished Cloth.—The manufacture of this kind of cloth is very simple, and may be carried on at very little expense. The cloth and linseed oil are the principal articles required for the establishment. Common canvas, of an open and coarse texture, is extended on large frames, placed under sheds, the sides of which are open, so as to afford a free passage to the external air. The manner in which the cloth is fastened to these frames is very simple and convenient, as, when it becomes slackened, during the application of the varnish-paste, it can be again tightened. It is fixed to each side of the frame by a kind of hooks, which catch the edge of the cloth, and by pieces of strong pack-thread passing through holes at the other extremity of the hooks, which are tied round movable pegs placed in the lower edge of the frame.

The mechanism by which the strings of a violin are stretched or unstretched, will give some idea of the arrangement of the pegs employed for extending the cloth in this apparatus. By these means the cloth can be easily stretched or relaxed, as the oily varnish may require, in the course of the operation. The whole being thus arranged, a liquid paste, made with drying oil, which may be varied at pleasure, is applied to the cloth.

Liquid Paste with Drying Oil.—Mix Spanish white or tobacco-pipe clay, or any other argillaceous matter, with water, and leave it at rest some hours, which will be sufficient to separate the argillaceous parts, and to produce a sediment. Stir the sediment with a broom, to complete the division of the earth; and after it has rested some seconds, decant the turbid water into an earthern or wooden vessel.

By this process the earth will be separated from the sand and other foreign bodies, which subside, and must be thrown away. If the earth has been washed by the same process, on a large scale, it is divided by kneading it. The supernatant water is thrown aside, and the sediment is placed in sieves, on pieces of cloth, where it is suffered to drain ; it is then mixed up with oil, rendered drying by a large proportion of litharge, that is to say, about a fourth of the weight of the oil. The consistence of thin paste being given to the mixture, it is spread over the cloth by means of an iron spatula, the length of which is equal to that of the breadth of the cloth. Though the earth is mixed in this manner still contains water, it readily unites with the boiled oil. The water passes into the tissue of the cloth, which facilitates its evaporation, and the cloth at the same time acquires the property of not becoming too much penetrated by the oily varnish.

However liquid the varnish may be, it does not transude to the inferior surface of the cloth. When the first stratum is dry, a second is applied. The inequalities produced by the coarseness of the cloth, or by an unequal extension of the paste, are smoothed down with a pumice-stone. The pumice-stone is reduced to powder and rubbed over the cloth with a piece of soft soap or cork dipped in water. A whole pumice-stone, one of the faces of which has been ground smooth, may also be employed.

The cloth must then be well washed in water to clean it ; and, after being suffered to dry, a varnish of gum lac, dissolved in linseed oil boiled with turpentine, and which is liquefied with oil of turpentine, if necessary, is then applied to it. This preparation produces yellowish-colored varnished cloth. When you are desirous of rendering it black, nothing will be necessary but to mix lamp-black with the Spanish white, or tobacco-pipe clay, which forms the basis of the liquid paste. Various shades of gray may be obtained according to the quantity of the lamp-black which is added. Amber and different ochrey argillaceous earths may be used to vary the tints, without causing any addition to the expense.

Fine printed varnished cloth.—The process just described for manufacturing common varnished and polished cloths, may serve to give some idea of that employed for making fine cloths of the same kind, decorated with a colored impression. At first this kind of manufacture was confined to common cloths with a smooth ground of different colors.

However, industry has given it a greater extent, by finding on the palette of the painter all those materials capable of making this art rival that of printed cloths. The firmness of the texture of the cloth, still increased by that of a pliable covering impermeable to water, has opened a very lucrative sale for this kind of manufacture, in consequence of a more careful application of the colors, which could be subjected to all the rules of design.

The Germans were the first to manufacture varnished cloths embellished with large and small objects, figures, and landscapes, and which, being designed for covering furniture subjected to daily use, gave certain support to this branch of industry.

This process, which is only an improvement of the

former, requires a finer paste, and cloth of a more delicate texture. The stratum of paste is applied in the same manner, and when dry and polished, the cloth is taken from the frame and removed to the painter's table, where the art of the colorist and designer is displayed under a thousand forms; and, as in that of printed cottons, exhibits a richness of tints and a distribution of subjects which discover taste and ensure a ready sale for the articles manufactured. The processes employed in these two arts to extract the coloring, are not the same.

In the art of cotton-printing, the colors are extracted by solution, as in that of dyeing. In printing varnished cloths, the coloring parts are the result of the union of drying oil mixed with varnish, and the different colors employed in oil painting or painting in varnish. The varnish applied to common oil-cloth is composed of gum lac and drying linseed oil; but that designed for printing varnished cloths requires some choice, both in regard to the oil and to the resinous matter which gives it consistence.

Prepared oil of poppy and copal form a pliable and solid varnish, possessing very little color. The unpleasant smell arising from oiled or varnished cloths, may be removed from them by simply exposing them to the action of a chlorine fumigation in a close room.

Varnished Silk.—There are two kinds of varnished silks—one employed for making umbrellas, coverings for hats, &c.—and the other, known under the name of "sticking-plaster," or "court-plaster." The first is prepared in the same manner as the varnished and polished cloths already described, but with some variation in the choice of the matters employed to make the liquid paste or varnish with which the silk is covered.

The basis of the second is a gelatinous stratum, which is afterwards covered with a varnish of the first class; that is, a spirituous varnish, very simple in its composition. For the preparation of the former, if the surface of the silk be pretty large, it is made fast to a wooden frame furnished with hooks and movable pegs, such as that used in the manufacture of common varnished cloths.

A certain quantity of soft paste, composed of linseed oil, boiled with a fourth part of litharge, Spanish white, or tobacco-pipe clay, lamp-black, and litharge, is then prepared in nearly the following proportions: Tobacco-pipe clay, dried and sifted through a silk-sieve, sixteen parts; litharge, ground with oil, dried and sifted in the same manner, three parts; lamp-black, one part. This paste is then spread in an uniform manner over the surface of the silk, by means of a long knife, having a handle at each extremity. In summer twenty-four hours are sufficient for its dessication. When dry, the knot produced by the inequalities of the silk, are smoothed with a pumice-stone.

This operation is performed with water; and, when finished, the surface of the silk is washed. It is then suffered to dry, and the copal varnish of the fifth class, No. 23, is applied. If it is intended to polish this var nish, it will be proper to apply a second stratum, after which it is polished with a ball of cloth and very fine tripoli, or with a piece of strong cloth only. The varnished silk which results from this process is very black, exceedingly pliable, and has a fine polish. It may be rumpled a thousand ways without retaining any fold, or the mark of a fold.

It is light; and this property renders it proper for coverings to hats, and for making cloaks and caps, so useful to travellers in the time of rain. When manufacturers wish to turn old remnants of silk to advantage, whatever may be their color, which do not exceed half a yard in length, they think it sufficient to fasten them to frames of the same size with a piece of packthread, keeping them as much stretched as possible. The liquid paste is then poured over the silk in small portions, and spread out by means of a common knife with a round point, somewhat like that of a table-knife, to prevent the cloth from being cut.

The handle of the knife stands at right angles to the blade, so that all the movements required for extending the paste can be made without the fingers touching the silk, and without removing the blade from an exactly horizontal position. A little practice will enable the workman to render the surface of the silk as smooth in this case as in that where a large blade is employed in the operation on a larger scale. In the last place, if the silk consists of long narrow bands, the mechanism employed for making two or three yards of plaster at once may be used. Provide a common smooth table, eighteen or twenty inches square, and placed perfectly horizontal At the two extremities of this table let there be fixed two iron screws in a perpendicular direction, which pass through two rings at the extremities of an iron rule, or blade, which stands in a vertical position, and which can be moved nearer to or further from the table by means of two nuts fitted to the screws. To determine the thickness of the stratum of the composition to be spread over the cloth, there are placed close to the screws, and between the rule and the table, as many squares cut from a common card as may be necessary to give the thickness required: two or three will be sufficient.

When this arrangement has been made, place the ends of the cloth between the rule and the table, in such a manner that it may pass beyond the former about an inch, that you may be able to draw it towards you during the operation; then pour the composition on the cloth near the interior side of the rule, in such a manner as to cover the cloth throughout its whole breadth.

Care must be taken to make the matter continue running, while another person draws the cloth towards him, till the whole length of it has been subjected to the pressure of the rule. By this mechanism the stratum will have an uniform thickness, and will be so even as to have no need of being smoothed with pumice-stone. When the stratum is dry, cover it with copal varnish, No. 23.

By pursuing a similar plan, and using a like composition, a beautiful article can be made of linen, felt, leather, &c., which is impermeable to water. It is thus that the patent glazed leather is made, which, when made into boots, half-boots, shoes, &c., constitute the most beautiful wearing apparel for the feet.

Another kind of Varnished Silk.—A kind of varnished silk, which has only a yellowish color, and which suffers the texture of the stuff to appear, has long been in use. The matter employed in the preparation of it is a plain varnish. The silk is covered with a mixture of three parts boiled oil of poppy, and one part of fat copal varnish, which is spread with a coarse brush, or with a knife.

Two coats are sufficient when the oil has been freed from its greasy principles over a slow fire, or when it has been boiled with a fourth part of its weight of litharge. The inequalities are removed by pumice-stone and water; after which the copal varnish is applied. This simple operation gives a yellowish color to white silk, which arises from the boiled oil and the varnish. This varnished silk possesses all those qualities ascribed to certain preparations of silk which are recommended to be worn as jackets by persons subject to rheumatism.

Court-Plaster.—The preparation of court-plaster is very simple: the basis of the first stratum is isinglass. Bruise a sufficient quantity of isinglass, and let it soak for twenty-four hours in a little warm water; expose it to heat over the fire, to dissipate the greater part of the water, and supply its place by proof spirit of wine, which will combine with the isinglass.

Strain the whole through a piece of open linen, and take care that the quantity of the solvent be such that on cooling it shall form a trembling jelly. Extend a piece of black silk on a wooden frame, and fix it in that position by means of tacks, or pack-thread; then with a brush made of badger's hair, apply the isinglass, after it has been exposed to a gentle heat, to render it liquid.

When this stratum is dry, which will soon be the case, apply a second, and then a third, if you are desirous of giving the plaster a certain degree of thickness. As soon as the whole is dry, cover it with two or three coats of strong tincture of balsam of Peru. This is the genuine "English court-plaster." It is pliable and never breaks—characters which distinguish it from so many other preparations sold under the same name.

This article has been adulterated as well as many others. A kind of plaster, the covering of which is very thick and brittle, is often sold under the same name. The fabricators of this article, instead of isinglass, which is dear, employ strong common glue, which they cover with spirituous varnish, like those of the first class.

This plaster cracks, and never has the balsamic odor by which the real English court-plaster is particularly characterized. To detect this fraud, nothing will be necessary but to rub it a little. When you wish to use the English plaster, moisten it with saliva, or warm water, on the side opposite to that which is varnished, and it will adhere quite close and fast. The adulterated plaster is too hard to adhere by so simple a preparation; it requires to be moistened on the varnished side.

Numerous processes for Staining Wood.

A Red Stain.—Take of

  Pearl-ash, ... 1 ounce.
  Brazil-wood, in chips, . . 1 pound.
  Water, ... 1 gallon.

Let them stand together two or three days, during which time the mixture should be frequently stirred; then boil it for two or three hours; and while boiling-hot, brush over the wood intended to be stained three or four times, or oftener, till the proper tint is obtained.

While wet, brush it over with a solution of alum in water, made in the proportion of two ounces of alum to a quart of water.

A light Red, approaching to Pink.—Add to a gallon of the above infusion two additional ounces of pearl-ash. The wood in this case should be often brushed over with the solution of alum. By increasing the quantity of pearl-ash, the red may be rendered still paler; but when more pearl-ash is added, a proportionate quantity of the solution of alum will also be required.

A very dark Red Stain.—Take of

  Salt of tartar, ... 1 ounce.
  Logwood, in chips, . . . ½ pound.
  Water, ... 2 quarts.

Boil the logwood chips in the water till it becomes of a very dark red color; then add the salt of tartar, and boil for two hours more. The decoction must be applied to the wood boiling-hot.

The old method of coloring wood red.—Dissolve one ounce of dragon's blood in one pint of rectified spirit of wine; brush the wood over with this varnish till it appears of the required color.

A Yellow Stain.—Take of

Turmeric-root, in powder,	1 ounce.
Rectified spirit of wine,	1 pint.

Digest for four days, shaking occasionally the mixture, when it may be strained off for use. Let it be applied to the wood by brushing it over three or four times, taking care that the first stain is dry before the second is applied. If the color be required of a reddish cast, a little dragon's blood may be added to the mixture.

Another Yellow Stain.—Take of

Alum,	½ ounce.
French berries,	1 pound.
Soft water,	1 gallon.

Boil them together for two hours, and while boiling brush over the wood with the decoction till it becomes of the required color. After the stain has been some hours applied, so that the wood is become quite dry, brush it over with a weak solution of alum-water.

Blue Stains.—Wood may be stained blue by either a solution of copper or of indigo. Copper will produce a bright color, and is more generally practicable.

A Blue Stain with Copper.—Dissolve copper-filings or slips in aqua-fortis, adding the filings or slips to the acid till all effervescence ceases: to the solution add of starch, finely powdered, the weight of one-fifth of the weight of the copper dissolved.

Make now a solution of pearl-ash in water; put as much of this solution to the solution of copper as will cause the copper to precipitate in a fine green powder. On the first addition of the pearl-ash solution, the liquid will appear of a dark muddy green; but by adding more of the pearl-ash solution, it will soon become clear, and the precipitate assumes a fine green color. The clear part must be poured off, and the precipitate washed in three or four quantities of clear water, till the water becomes tasteless.

Let the precipitate be dried for use; which is, in fact, a "*verditer.*" After the wood intended to be stained has been brushed over in a similar way, as described for other colors, till it is stained a dark green, make a solution consisting of two ounces of pearl-ash in a pint of water, and brush it over the wood boiling-hot, when it will appear of a fine deep blue color.

A Green Stain.—This may be made with the same precipitate of any tint, by merely melting the solution of pearl-ash, and brushing the mixture over the wood once or more, according to the required tint.

A Blue Stain with Indigo.—Dissolve indigo in sulphuric acid, or a liquid blue may be thus prepared: Put three ounces of indigo, in powder, to one pound of sulphuric acid. When the indigo is dissolved, which it will be in about twenty-four hours, provided the mixture has been occasionally stirred, add to the solution one pint of boiling water. This solution must be applied to the wood boiling-hot. Dissolve by boiling three ounces of cream of tartar in a quart of water; with this solution, used copiously, brush over the wood before the moisture of the indigo is quite absorbed.

A Purple Stain.—Take of

    Brazil-wood, in chips, . 4 ounces.
    Logwood chips, ... 1 pound.
    Water, ... 1 gallon.

Boil these together for two or three hours. The decoction must be applied boiling-hot. When dry, brush it over with a solution containing a quarter of an ounce of pearl-ash to half a gallon of water. This solution must be carefully used, as it gradually changes its color from a brown-red, which it originally is, to a dark blue purple, and therefore its effects must be carefully noted to make the desired color.

A Black Stain.—Brush the wood several times with the hot decoction of logwood described in the last article, omitting the Brazil-wood; next prepare an infusion thus:

    Take of powdered galls, 4 ounces.
    Water, ... 2 quarts.

Place them in a gentle heat for three or four days; brush the wood over with this infusion three or four times, and then pass over the wood again with a solution composed of two ounces of sulphate of iron, and a quart of water.

A very fine Black, can be produced by brushing the wood several times with a solution of copper in aquafortis, and afterwards with the decoction of logwood, which must be repeated till the desired color is obtained, and then the greenness of the copper wholly overcome.

A common Black Stain, is produced by immersing a pound of iron nails into half a gallon of vinegar, with a small quantity of verdigris. This is the common black stain for chairs; it is also useful to mix with colors that require grain, as rosewood, tulip, &c.

Mahogany Stains.—These stains are very useful, and if well prepared and applied to suitable wood, resemble red mahogany.

A Light-Red Brown Mahogany.—Take of

Fustic chips,	4 ounces.
Madder-root, in powder,	½ pound.
Water,	1 gallon.

Boil together for two or more hours. This decoction must be applied to the wood boiling-hot, till the proper color is obtained. If the grain of the wood be not sufficiently varied, a varnish brush, dipped in the black stain and passed lightly over the wood while wet, will greatly improve it, and give it the appearance of dark Honduras mahogany.

A fine Mahogany Stain, is produced by mixing the tincture of dragon's blood and turmeric-root in spirit of wine. By diminishing or increasing the proportion of each of the ingredients, the brown stain may be varied to a more red or yellow cast at pleasure.

Spanish Mahogany Stain.—Take of

    Madder-root, in powder, . ½ pound.
    Fustic chips, ... 1 ounce.
    Logwood chips, ... 2 ounces.
    Water, ... 1 gallon.

Boil for two or three hours. Apply the decoction boiling-hot. When the wood has been brushed over several times, and is become dry, let it be slightly brushed over with a solution of a quarter of an ounce of pearl-ash in a quart of water. Any stain of intermediate colors may be made by varying the proportion of the ingredients.

Fancy Woods.—The preceding stains may, by judicious management, be combined in various ways, so as to represent many variegated woods. Rosewood in particular may thus be imitated.

Rosewood Stains.—The articles chiefly stained to imitate rosewood are chairs, which are commonly for such purposes made of beech. They are usually dipped in a large copper containing the boiling red stain, then taken out and dried before they are dipped again. When the red stain is acquired, a flat varnish-brush, having its hairs separated, is dipped in the black stain, and drawn over the chairs which are stained red.

The application of some polish to such woods as have just been given, is necessary to render them pleasing to the eye.

To make Sweet Oil Turps without smell.—Half a gallon of gray stone lime, slack it properly, in five and a half gallons of water to destroy its property, then put it into a can, shaking it three or four times a day, leaving the cork out. Let it properly settle, then pour off the water from the lime, which will be oily, then add raw linseed oil five and a half pints, shaking it three or four times; after this add quarter of a pint of clarified vitriol to each gallon: it is then fit for use.

To Varnish Prints.—Dissolve one ounce of the best isinglass in a pint of water by boiling it over the fire; strain it through fine muslin, and keep it for use. Try this size on a piece of paper, moderately warm; if it glistens, it is too thick: add more water. If it soaks into the paper, it is too thin. Add or diminish the isinglass till it merely dulls the surface. Give the print two or three coats, letting it dry between each; bear lightly on your brush, which should be a flat tin camel's hair, then with best mastic varnish, give it two or three coats.

To polish on Paint.—Two and a half ounces of spirit of wine, one drachm of oil of almonds, one drachm of gum elemi, half an ounce of orange shellac, pounded fine, and put altogether into a bottle to dissolve; when dissolved, rub it on with soft woollen or cotton wadding.

OBSERVATIONS ON HOUSE-PAINTING, WITH INSTRUCTIONS FOR PREPARING THE VARIOUS COLORS, &c.

It is quite necessary, to make the work satisfactory, for the operator to have vessels that are clean, as also the brushes, cans, &c., that he may need in the course of his work; such as his various paint-pots or vessels to mix his color in, or use it from. They are occasionally bought at the shops, nicely made of stout tin, and such are easily kept clean, and save their expense in color, which is easily brushed down their smooth sides: marble slab and muller, to grind the finer colors used in painting with.

A small cast-iron mill is useful sometimes, not only to grind colors, but to pass the tinted color through, so that it may be more thoroughly mixed. It is scarcely necessary to say that it is presumed the workman will know what brushes he will require, according to the work he has in hand. His large ground paint-brush, called a "pound-brush;" his half-size, for smaller work, as blinds, shutters, &c.; fitch and sash tools, duster, pallet, putty, and hack-knives; oval and flat varnish brushes, varnish-pot; step-ladders and long ladders, mahl-stick, pallet-board, gilding-knife, camel and sable hair-pencils, whitewash brush, sometimes his Jack, for window work, cushion and tip-pole, &c.

As a general thing, it is best to buy putty at a regular color store, where you may depend upon its being made of good dry whiting and linseed oil, and should be freely and carefully used after the work has had one coat of paint, for the fresh paint holds the putty very firmly. White lead is to be judged of by being well ground and possessing the mellowness given to it by age.

It is thought that the best article is the most economical, as it works out with more ease, and repays the difference of cost in its appearance. Linseed oil is also better for having due age, for the same reasons as the white lead, working with softness and advantage after parting with the water, which is generally combined with new oil.

YELLOW.

Yellow Ochre.—When good, a very durable color; it has a good pleasing tint with white. The French is the best and most economical, taking up less oil, and preserving its color in oil much better than the American.

Chrome Yellow.—A bright, durable color, of different shades, and exceedingly useful, of great strength, and has superseded the use of patent and king's yellow, from its facility of working and cheapness. *Dutch Pink* is mostly used in distemper for wall-work, and has little or no body in oil. *Stone Yellow* is not much used by house-painters; a cleaner tint than yellow ochre, and sometimes useful in greens.

BLUES.

Chinese Blue is a soft Prussian blue; it makes a rich tint, is very strong, and easily ground in water or oil. *Ultramarine* is now so cheaply imitated as to bring it into general use for any fancy work, ornamenting walls, &c.; a brilliant and enduring color, with very little body, it makes a rich appearance when strewed on like smalts. *Prussian Blue*, from its strength and comparative cheapness, is used most in tinting green and white. *Indigo* is little used in oil, but good in distemper or water colors. *Antwerp Blue* is similar to Prussian blue, and not so green in tint. *Refiner's and Verditer Blues* are copper colors, useful in water colors. *Blue Smalts* are used in sign-work, to strew over the fresh paint after the gilt letters are cut in, or pointed around.

BLACKS.

Lamp-Black, either calcined, or in a crude state, is the most usual black for house-painting, and the difference in their use well repays the additional cost of the calcined, and is best purchased ready ground in boiled linseed oil, to assist its drying.

Blue Black is a variety useful in tinting the white.

Ivory and Drop Blacks are much used in finer works, to produce more intense blacks, as carriages, wagons, &c.

WHITES.

China White.—A fine variety of flake white, and better than the generality of Cremnitz white; is used very generally, ground in white hard copal, and painted on in several coats, to prepare a ground for polishing; or, ground in Damar varnish, is brushed evenly and smoothly over the work, which requires to be finished beforehand in spirit color, and then painted twice with the varnish color, and brushed quickly in the last coating, to leave it glossy.

Paris White is much used in finishing fine ceilings, after they are well cleaned, and prepared with a thin coat of lime.

Kalsomine, a white silky powder, is used with gelatine to finish ceilings and side walls. After it has been used some time, the gelatine perishes, and, if the work be varnished, flakes off. Lime-washes must not be put on over size preparations, as they cause the work to flake off.

REDS.

Carmine is the most superb red in common use, and is serviceable in tinting wall-work, if the ground be duly prepared, first, with Indian red and white; secondly, with white and a good lake; and lastly, with white and carmine, prepared with dry China white, a little soft white varnish and spirits of turpentine, so as to work evenly. Good lake makes the next best reddish tint, used as the carmine, only substituting lake in place of the carmine in the last tint.

Indian Red.—A permanent and very useful color as a ground for the above colors, in wall-work, and also for vermilion in carriage or other work.

Chinese Vermilion.—Also used as a finishing tint for rooms, where lakes and carmines are too expensive, and in a variety of ornamental work.

French Vermilion, a richer and more scarlet tint, is much used in ornamental work.

English Pale Vermilion is used as above in carriage work, and fine ornaments: beautiful in tint and an excellent body.

Trieste.—A good article, not quite so rich as the last mentioned, but useful from its body and cheaper price.

Persian Red and American Vermilion are good cheap priming colors.

Orange Mineral is a rich preparation like red lead, used in the ground with white lead, and also to mix with Venetian red, to improve its color and cause it to dry.

Red Lead, a similar color, used on iron work, and with Venetian red, as above, and as a dryer in boiling oil: a very useful red paint.

Rose Pink is a rich color, which answers well under copal varnish or inside work. *Venetian Red* is a good iron color, used on houses outside and on brick work, and sometimes on roofs of houses, as it is a lasting rich red. *Spanish Brown* is a common dark red color, for ordinary rough outside work. These two last are much better to be obtained of the pure iron color, as the common or clayey varieties absorb so much oil, and do not endure like the best.

GREENS.

Chrome Green.—A strong color will bear four pounds of white lead to one pound, and make a good color. The tone can be varied by adding chrome yellow or Prussian blue.

Paris Green, called also sweinfurt and emerald green. A beautiful color, covers indifferently, is best prepared ground fine in boiled oil. The work must be carefully primed with a similar tint, then painted twice with this green, and if it does not gloss well, a thin coat must be floated over, mixed with copal varnish.

Verdigris is little used now, except with boiled oil on vessels, or with resin varnish on inside blinds or common bedsteads. It is mixed one pound to three of white lead in the oil, and one to four in the varnish, and can be had ground in oil at the shops.

There are various low-priced greens, sold both dry and ground in oil, at the shops, such as Brunswick, Imperial, Saxon, Prussian, &c., &c., used in place of chrome green on cheap work.

BROWNS.

Umber is the most useful and cheapest brown color, both raw and burnt. The latter is a very rich and deep tint, and makes pleasant drab colors with white. Umber is a most excellent dryer, and is put into oil with litharge and red lead when about to be boiled.

Vandyke Brown is useful in tints and in veining imitations of wood and marble.

Purple Brown.—A strong color, and makes a rich stone color, with yellow ochre and white.

Raw Sienna.—A fine yellow brown, useful in imitations, either in water or oil.

Burnt Sienna.—A fine red brown, useful in tinting, and also in imitating mahogany.

Welsh Umber.—A soft color, used in water.

The colors above named are best bought ground in oil or water, or levigated; for being earthy colors, they have naturally more or less sand with them.

In grinding any of them upon the slab, have them well pulverized, and stir the oil into it, till it is just wet. Then with the pallet-knife put on the centre of the slab about two spoonsful at once, and placing the muller upon it, turn it around two or three times, and if you think it too dry, drop a few drops of oil on it; then proceed to rub it around the stone, bearing hard on the muller, so as to crush it finely, until you find it quite smooth, when it is to be scraped up with the pallet-knife towards the centre, and lifted with the same knife into the vessel for use. If there be more than is needed, it can be kept in bladder.

In preparing to paint a good dwelling, after having obtained the necessary colors and brushes, see that you have a few pounds of good pumice-stone, a quire or two of assorted sand-paper, to smooth the inequalities in the work; some twenty pounds of putty, to stop up after the first coat, in every part of the house; a sufficiency of fine slacked lime, and a proper number of large and small vessels, to mix the colors in and use it from; a few pounds of soaked glue, &c.

If the wood work be new, and no wall work required, you will go over it carefully with a small brush, and some of the glue-size, colored with red lead, covering what knots and stains may appear in the wood, after which the priming coat, of almost all oil, and good white lead, tinted with Indian red, should be evenly brushed over the work; and, as soon as dry, the putty-knife and putty should follow, to stop all the cracks and nail holes. Then should follow the second coat, with a little spirits of turpentine in the oil, and the color slightly tinged with blue black. This is generally thought sufficient for the attic and third stories. But the rest of the house is usually finished with old ground white lead, thinned with spirits of turpentine. The roof, if covered with tin, should be painted once in three years. There are many different methods in use. Some paint with raw oil, dry Spanish brown, and a little red lead, to dry it, for fear of a rain: others, with Spanish brown, more red lead, and half whale oil with the linseed oil; others use yellow ochre and Black, mixed in the same oils; others use a roof paint, made by boiling paint skins in whale oil, and carefully straining them while warm, reserving the remaining skins, to stop the leaks around chimneys and dormer windows. This last mentioned paint is probably serviceable from its elasticity. In the country, many paint their roofs and outbuildings in the same way, using sometimes Venetian red from its brightness.

If the work is required to be painted in oil, it must be carefully cleaned from dirt and grease, the lumps and roughness smoothed down with pumice and sand-paper, and an even coat of white, tinted with Indian red and mixed half oil and half spirits, carefully put on, and when dry, all the cracks and crevices, fairly puttied up.

The ceilings and side walls should be first brushed off, and one thin coat of lime passed over the ceiling. If the side walls are to be painted, a thin sizing of glue water should be evenly passed over it, and the priming coat, half oil and half spirits, brushed smoothly over it. The ceiling should be finished with a coat of Paris white, mixed with clear water, in which a little alum is dissolved. In the attics it is usual to finish the side walls with two coats, the last coat mixed with one-third boiled oil and the rest spirits of turpentine, tinting them more deeply than the walls of the other stories. The same process is to be observed in the other stories, except that if the third or finishing coat is to dry glossy, the second coat should have less oil, that it may dry without gloss; and the last coat, boiled oil and spirits of turpentine, as directed above. If the last coat should be dead, without gloss, then the second coat should dry with a gloss, being mixed half oil and half spirits, and finished with all spirits, mixed with old white lead, so that it may work smoothly. The ground and second coat tints should correspond in tone with the last color required, and care taken not to make them too dark.

TINTING.

Lead Color is to be made with blue black and lampblack, heightened with indigo or Prussian blue.

Lilac made with the same tints, and purple lake or Indian red.

Flesh Color is made with lakes, carmine, and a little blue, with some yellow.

Buff Color is made with a little chrome yellow, yellow ochre, and white.

Carnations, of carmine or scarlet lake, and the best and clearest dry white. Perhaps the Damar varnish, used so as to dry without gloss, would be the best vehicle for such delicate colors, in which carmines and lakes are used.

Orange.—Vermilion and chrome yellow, and cheaper orange mineral and Indian red.

Bronze Green.—Chrome green, subdued with burnt umber.

Olive.—Umber and fine yellow ochre, or stone ochre. Where the ochre predominates mixed with white, a fine Portland stone color is obtained.

Freestone Color.—Made with purple, brown, yellow ochre, and a little blue black and white.

Chocolate Color.—Spanish brown, or Venetian red and black.

Claret.—Indian red and blue black, glazed over with a deep crimson lake.

Drabs of a great variety may be made with raw and burnt siennas, Vandyke brown, Indian red, and raw and burnt umbers.

GILDING IN OIL.

This is best done on solid and smooth painted ground, of a gray tint, so hard as to be rubbed down smooth. The oil-size is made of Oxford ochre and chrome yellow, finely ground in fat oil, and tempered with boiled oil, so as to dry in twenty-four hours, and hold its tach for double that time. It should be used with a sable or camel's hair pencil or brush, to leave its surface smooth and glossy. In sizing letters on a sign-board, the shape of the letter is to be made fuller than it is to be finished, so that there may be room to work around the gilt letters with the ground-work, to leave the edge smooth.

When the size is dry, so as to feel tachy, and leave no impression of the finger, it is ready for the gold-leaf, which is put thereon in various ways. Some, folding back the paper leaf, run the fore-finger nail along its edge, and, turning it suddenly over against the sized surface, so much of the gold remains, and is pressed down evenly with a piece of cotton, or large camel's hair-brush; others, with a sharp knife cut entirely through the book, dividing it into the required strips, and put it on in a similar way to the last. The neatest and best plan is to use the Gilder's Cushion, where the full leaf of gold is thrown on, and laid flat with the knife and breath, and, being cut into requisite size, lifted up with the lip, and put upon the work, then pressed down with a camel's hair or fitch hair-brush. This has many advantages, avoiding any injury to the work, by improperly pressing it, and being enabled to cut the gold without waste—points certainly very desirable to be obtained.

OF COMPOUND COLORS.

These are formed by mixing two only, and will be the best and the richest.

Size.—The best size for distemper colors is made from the clippings of the skin of animals, which must be submitted to strong boiling. Take the quantity necessary, put it into an iron kettle, and fill it with water; let it stand twenty-four hours, till the pieces are thoroughly soaked. Let the size boil five hours, occasionally taking off the scum.

When it is sufficiently boiled, take it from the fire, and strain it through a coarse cloth. If the size is to be kept for a length of time, dissolve two or three pounds of alum in boiling water, and add to every pail ful. The size must then be boiled again till it becomes very strong: it must be strained a second time, put into a cool place, and it will keep good several months.

Brilliant Peach Blossom.—Orange lead (orpiment) and whiting, when properly mixed, composes a beautiful and unfading color; it is much used by paper-stainers. Dissolve whiting in water; then grind very fine in water a small quantity of orange lead, and mix with the whiting; add sufficient size to the mixture, and strain it through a sieve, and put into a cool place till fit for use.

This color must be worked in a jelly, as the orange lead is heavy, and would otherwise separate from the other parts and sink to the bottom in a pure state.

Salmon Color.—An excellent salmon color can be made by dissolving whiting in water, and tinging it with the best English Venetian red, finely ground in water. A little Venetian red mixed with lime whitewash, and a proportionate quantity of alum, will answer very well for common purposes. It is important, when English red is required, that you obtain it genuine, as a spuriou article is frequently sold for it, which, when used, spoil the intended effect when applied to fine with.

Pink.—Dissolve in water, separately, whiting and rose pink, mix them to the texture required: strain the color through a sieve, and bind with size.

Lilac.—Take a small quantity of indigo finely ground in water, and mix it with whiting till it produces a dark gray; then add to the mixture some rose pink. Well mix and strain the color, and a beautiful lilac will be the result.

Light Gray.—A small quantity of lamp-black mixed with whiting, composes a gray; more or less black, of course, regulates the shade. With whiting, therefore, mixed with black in varying proportions, a wide range of shades may be obtained, from the darkest to the lightest gray.

French Gray.—Whiting predominates in this color: it is treated as the other grays, but with this difference, that it admits of lake instead of black. Take the quantity, therefore, of whiting necessary, and soak it in water, then add the Prussian blue and lake, which has been finely ground in water. The quantity of each of those colors should, of course, be proportioned to the warmth of color required. This is a handsome and delicate color for walls. Either of the preceding grays will answer for the first coat, as the French gray will cover upon it very well. Rose pink may be substituted, but it does not make so brilliant a color, neither is it so durable.

Orange Color.—For walls and stables. Use two pounds of green copperas, dissolved in hot water, just sufficient to dissolve it. Mix it well with eight gallons of fresh lime-wash. Stir it well while using.

Another.—This is a mixture of whiting, French yellow, or Dutch pink and orange lead. Those ingredients may be proportioned according to taste. This color cannot be worked except in a size-jelly, as the orange lead is a color which has great body.

Buff.—A good buff may be produced by dissolving separately whiting and French yellow in water. A little English Venetian red must be added to give the yellow a warm cast. Mix with size, and strain as before directed.

An excellent Green for Walls.—Take two pounds of mineral green, and six pounds of good green verditer; mix them together, and grind in water: mix with size, and work the color when it has formed a jelly. This green has a good body, and is very durable.

Another.—Mix a solution of common salt and blue vitriol in water; by putting copper-plates therein, a green precipitate will be gradually formed, which may be mixed with whiting, and then spread on a board to dry.

Another ; good and cheap.—Take eight pounds of Roman vitriol and two pounds of whiting, boil them in a brass or copper kettle in three gallons of water one hour, stirring the mixture the whole time till thoroughly dissolved. Pour it into an earthen pan, and let it stand several days. Decant the water, and mix the sediment with size; apply it to the walls with a whitewash-brush. The shade may be altered or improved by adding a little

Dutch pink or chrome yellow. When required for use, it must be dissolved in water, mixed with size, &c.

This color must not come in contact with iron, as the Roman vitriol powerfully attacks it, and thereby spoils the color.

Blue in Distemper.—A good blue is made by dissolving whiting in water, and mixing some indigo with it.

Blue Verditer.—The best blue in use for distemper colors on walls. Dissolve some pieces of copper in aqua-fortis, and when dissolved, produce a precipitation of it by adding quick-lime, in such doses that it will be entirely absorbed by the acid. In order that the precipitate may be pure copper without any mixture, when the liquor has been decanted, wash the precipitate, and spread it out on a piece of linen cloth to drain. If a portion of this precipitate, which is green, be placed on a grinding-stone, and a little quick lime in powder be added, the green color will be changed into a beautiful blue. The proportion of lime added is from seven to ten parts in a hundred. As the whole matter has already acquired the consistency of paste, dissication soon takes place.

Straw Color in Size.—Dissolve the necessary quantity of whiting in water, then grind in water some chrome yellow or Dutch pink. Mix to the shade required, and add some strong size. Strain the color through a hair-sieve, and set it in a cool place till fit for use.

Drab, in Size.—An excellent drab. Dissolve in water, whiting, and grind some burnt umber very fine in water. Mix it to the shade required. Strain the color as usual, and mix with size. Raw umber will make a drab of a different shade.

Another.—Dissolve separately some whiting and French yellow in water. Take a proportionate quantity of each, and mix them together till a bright yellow is produced. Grind a little lamp-black very fine in vinegar, and with it sufficiently stain the color to form a drab; another shade may be obtained by adding a little Venetian red. Thus, by diversifying the proportions of the above mentioned pigments, a great variety of shades may be produced.

Milk Paint for out-door work.—The quantity for one hundred square feet: One quart of skimmed milk, three ounces of lime, two ounces of linseed or poppy oil, one pound and a half of Spanish white or whiting. Put the lime into a clean bucket, add sufficient of the milk to slake the lime, add the oil a few drops at a time, stirring the mixture with a flat stick till the whole of the oil is incorporated in the mass; then add the remainder of the milk, and afterwards the Spanish white or whiting, finely powdered, and sifted gently over the mixture by degrees. Curded milk will do for the purpose, but it must not be sour. One coat of this will do for ceilings and staircases in general; two coats or more for new wood. Where color is required, you may use powdered umber, ochres, chromes, greens, blues, pinks, &c., &c.,

ground in milk. For particular work strain the color through a hair-sieve.

For out-door work.—Eight ounces of lime newly slacked, by dipping it in water, and allowing it to break down in the open air. Now take two ounces of burgundy pitch, and dissolve by a gentle heat in six ounces of poppy or linseed oil; then add to the hot lime two quarts of skimmed milk while in a hot state. Add the mixture of pitch and oil a little at a time, stirring all the while. Lastly, add three pounds of powdered whiting.

To Whiten Ceilings or Walls.—Take the best whiting and break down in water, then boil some parchment-cuttings three hours, and strain off the liquor after the whole is mixed together. London size will be a good substitute for the above; if the double size, use nearly half water; if the single, use none. You must test the size, as some is much stronger than others. You may add a small piece of blue-black to the whiting, and before using this wash you may stir in a little turpentine.

Distemper Colors for Walls.—If distemper is to be applied to a wall or ceiling which is covered with plaster, some whiting is put into water, where it may be easily broken and diluted if allowed time to soak; it must be completely saturated, and when it has settled, the clear water must be poured off. To correct the too great whiteness, and to prevent a yellow cast, grind separately in some water a little indigo or ivory-black, and mix with it; then add to the mixture some strong size which has been previously warmed, well stirring the whole till properly mixed. The whole of the distemper must be strained while warm, in order to remove all impurities and thoroughly mix the color. When this is done, the distemper may be put into a cool place till it is formed into a weak, trembling jelly, which is the only proper state in which to apply it to the walls. All size distemper colors which are applied to walls, and which are mixed with whiting, should at all times be worked cold, and of a weak, trembling jelly, otherwise it will be impossible to make good work, and great care should be taken not to have too much body in the color, for it will certainly crack and fall off in scales, as it is not the strength of the size that causes the work to crack, but the body of color. There is a great advantage in having a sufficient quantity of size in the first coat of distemper, as it binds hard, and stops the suction of the wall, in consequence of which the next coat, if properly prepared, will not move the first strata, but it will work perfectly free, and when dry, the work will have a uniform and solid appearance. If these instructions are fully attended to, the amateur cannot fail in his endeavors to execute his work in the best manner. This method of whitewashing and coloring walls is far superior to lime, as it works much smoother, and when properly mixed and worked upon a new wall, it will not crack and fall off in scales; it also covers better, and after being repeatedly applied for a number of years, the walls need no scraping, as the color easily washes off with a whitewashing brush, after they have been well soaked with water.

Lime Whitewash.—Lime whitewash is made from lime well slacked. Dissolve two pounds and a half of alum in boiling water, and add it to every pailful of whitewash. Lime whitewash should be used very thin, and when it is sufficiently bound on the wall by means of alum, two thin coats will cover the work better; this may be used for the first coat, thinned with water. Most whitewashers apply their wash too thick, and do not mix a proportionate quantity of alum to bind it, consequently the operation of the brush rubs off the first coat in various parts and leaves an uneven surface, and the original smooth surface of the wall is entirely destroyed.

To make Paste for Paper-hanging.—Mix four pounds of flour well with cold water, as thick as you can, then boil two gallons of water and add a little alum, then take a little of the hot water and mix with that you have stirred with the cold water, stirring the while till you have added the whole, then strain for use. Thin it with cold water. Size your walls with thin glue-size.

Color to imitate Cherry-Tree.—Grind raw and burnt terradasienna with whiting, then to one gallon of water add half a pound of glue; let the water be warm to dissolve the glue. When the color is applied, it will do with or without varnish.

Transparent Colors for Painting.—The best are made from vegetable or animal substances; minerals do not work so well with water, and are apt to fade.

Directions for inside Painting.—The first thing is to have the room free from dust; the next essential thing is to kill the knots of the wood. When the work is knotted, proceed to prime it, which must be made to dry exceedingly hard, in order to stop the unction of the wood, otherwise the second coat will, by the operation of the brush, rub off the priming in different parts of the work, and there will be no uniformity in the finishing coat, but it will leave some parts dead and others of a shining surface. The middle coat may be of size color applied warm; use but little color in your size or it will scale.

To prepare knotting, grind some lead-powder in water, and mix it with strong glue-size: put it into an iron vessel, and when used it must be applied to the knots with a brush quite warm. To make priming, mix or grind red and white lead with linseed oil; then, for the dryers, take a little litharge and burnt white vitriol, or patent dryers, which must be ground on a slab very fine in turpentine. Mix them altogether, and thin with boiled oil.

The burnt vitriol and litharge act, as it were, in opposition to each other, and render the paint exceedingly drying; and the turpentine, with the boiled oil, prevents the color from running down the quicks of the work. When the priming is dry, fill up the nail-holes and crevices with putty. Rub the surface of the work smooth with glass-paper, and dust it well.

The Second Coat for White.—If this coat is intended as a finish, too much oil must not be added, or the work will turn yellow. Mix the white lead in raw linseed oil, with equal parts of oil and turps and a little litharge; but it does not require so much as in the priming, as it will dry in a little time if the first coat is hard. The white may be heightened with a little lamp-black or Prussian blue.

The Third Coat.—If this coat is intended to have but little gloss, the white lead must be mixed in linseed oil, but not too stiff, and thinned with spirits of turpentine, adding to it a little litharge and burnt white vitriol, and also a very small portion of lamp-black. For white: If a dead white is required for the finishing coat, the white lead must be ground as stiff as possible in linseed oil, and made quite thin with spirits of turpentine, which requires no driers. A small portion of lamp-black may be added to heighten the white, and ground exceedingly fine and strained.

Painting in Dead Colors for Inside Work.—If the work is to be painted in a superior manner, new wood requires three coats of oil color and a flat, as the flat is not intended to give body to the work, but is a thin wash, merely to beautify and give a smooth, solid, and uniform appearance; and to apply this last coat, which is generally about the third day after the last coat of oil paint, as the flatting will then appear soft. If the last coat of oil paint remains to get hard, the flatting will appear harsh and streaky. The proper method of flatting a door is to begin and finish the panels, taking care to cut them in clean; proceed with the styles, working the color quick, in order to keep it from setting before the door is finished; and if the flatting should set on any part of the work, it must be rubbed up with fresh color as you proceed to finish, otherwise it will not have an uniform appearance.

To Flat a French Gray on hard-finished Walls.—In painting a new wall, the oil should be put on quite warm, in order to make the paint adhere; without this precaution the paint would be apt to rise and fall off in scales. The first coat to be applied to the wall is good boiled oil; when this is dry and hard, a thin coat of weak size may be put on tinged with red lead, in order to stop the suction of the wall, and bring the work to an uniform appearance. When this second coat is dry, the wall must be painted with a thin coat of light lead color, mixed in boiled oil, to which a little spirits of turpentine and litharge must be added to harden it. When this coat is dry, rub it smooth with sand-paper, procure some of the best English ground lead, and mix it with equal parts of raw linseed oil and spirits of turpentine; then, to form the French gray, stain the white paint with Prussian blue, and tinge it with vermilion to give it a warm appearance; some burnt white vitriol must also be added to give it a drying quality. Strain the color through a coarse cloth, or a sieve made of fine wire. When it has stood three or four days, the work will be in good order for flatting; but before this is put on, the work should be lightly rubbed with sand-paper, and well dusted.

To make and apply the Flatting.—Mix the best English ground white lead with spirits of turpentine to the thickness of treacle, put in Prussian blue, finely ground, in equal parts of oil and turpentine. To make a superb gray, lake must be substituted for vermilion. Great care must be taken to match the shade of the last coat, by comparing the flatting with the remains of the last color which may have been left in the paint-pot. It should be observed that the flatting must be made about one-third lighter, as the ground-color will not be so apt to show through, and it will, therefore, give the work a more solid appearance. When the flatting is brought to the proper shade, strain it, and thin it to the proper consistency for use. Good, soft-spreading brushes must be used, otherwise it will be impossible to make good work. If the wall be from eight to ten feet high, it will require two men to flat it. Fix a scaffold from one end of the wall to the other, a proper depth from the ceiling, in order to reach with care the top of the work. Let the color be properly thinned and stirred from the bottom, and be careful to have everything provided, as you cannot leave off work till one flank is finished. The bottom of the wall must be commenced first, painting not more than twelve or eighteen inches wide at one time. Move the brush in a perpendicular direction, and when you have painted as high as you can conveniently reach, carefully cross the work with a light hand, in order to give the color an uniform extension. When this is done, finish the work by laying it off very lightly, beginning at the bottom and striking the brush up about a foot, then from the top lightly draw the brush to the bottom. When this is done, the man on the plank must begin where the other left off, and finish the top. In the meantime the man on the floor must begin another width, and so proceed till one side of the wall is finished.

N. B.—The same precaution will be highly necessary in flatting every other color.

Instructions for Writing, with the Colors to be used for the Ground and Letters.—On an oak ground, ornamental letters, in ultramarine blue, filled in with gold and silver leaf, blocked up and shaded with burnt sienna.

Another.—Gold letters on a white marble ground, blocked and shaded with a transparent brown or burnt sienna.

On glass: Gold letters, shaded with burnt sienna.

Another.—Gold letters, shaded with black, on a scarlet or chocolate ground.

On a rich blue ground, gold letters, double shaded, black and white.

White letters on a blue ground, shaded with black, looks very well.

On a purple ground, pink letters shaded with white.

Mix ultramarine and vermilion for a ground-color, white letters, shaded with a light gray.

Vermilion ground, chrome yellow stained with vermilion and lake for the letters, shaded black. A substitute for the above colors: Rose pink and red lead; and for the letters, stone yellow, white lead, and Venetian red.

A good substitute for gold is obtained by grinding white lead, chrome yellow, and a dust of vermilion together. Mix your colors for writing in boiled oil, and use for driers gold size.

Before writing, set or mark out your work with a piece of chalk, pipe-clay, charcoal or pencil, as the color of the ground may require. Let your capital letters be a little higher than the others, and the person's name the largest on the board, the trade next in size to the name.

In preparing your board for writing, let your color be well strained, and mix in linseed oil with the addition of a little boiled oil to give a gloss. Always wash your board with clean water before writing it. If it be for gold letters, and the board is stickey from being recently painted, take the white of an egg, and as much cold water, well mixed together, and with a sponge or clean tool, go all over the surface with it. Let it get quite dry, and go over the same with powdered whiting, and afterwards brush off all you can. This is to prevent your gold sticking to the board; be sure to let none of the yolk of the egg mix with the white. When you have written in gold-size about a dozen letters, try if the first be ready to gild: this may be known by the touch of the finger; if it is a little stickey, it is ready. To gild: Lay on the gold from your book as carefully as possible, by gently pressing it to the letters leaf after leaf, with care not to rumple it; then brush off with a piece of cotton wool or hare's tail, or some other soft substance, all the loose bits, mending the holes, if any, with the same. The pencils used in this work are of camel's hair of various lengths and sizes.

In using gold or silver leaf, when applied from your book, press it up gently with your piece of cotton wool.

Other good grounds for gold letters are: blues, vermilion, lakes, and saxon.

To give Lustre to a Light Blue Ground.—After the letters are written and dry, paint the ground over again between the letters with the same color, and while wet, take pulverized Prussian blue and sift over the surface; glass, frost, or smalts, may be used instead of or with the blue. When dry, brush off the loose particles.

Harmony of Colors.—Red looks well with blacks, whites, or yellows.

Blues harmonize with whites and yellows.

Greens, with whites, black or yellow.

Gold, with blacks or browns.

White appears well with any color.

Purple, pink and white, &c., &c.

For Marbling Paper.—Mix a solution of gum tragacanth, prepared as follows: The gum is of a pale white transparent color; a pure white is not so good, nor is the gum of a brownish color so good. Soak the gum in water fifty hours, one-quarter of a pound to three gallons of water; strain it through a fine hair-sieve or cloth; when reduced to the thickness of gum used in miniature painting, to be well stirred up when used. Then pour the above into a wooden trough, about two inches and a half larger each way than the sheets of paper. Commence work by sprinkling the color into the trough, which must be full of the solution mixed with equal parts of ox-gall and oil of turpentine, having a brush in each separate color, then thin it with a little clean water. When you throw your spots in, if they spread too much, the color has too much gall in; if they contract again after spreading, there is not enough gall in. To prepare the paper for use dip it in water over night; if in sheets, lay them on each other, and place a weight upon them. In using the paper, take hold of it at angles of the corners, and place it on the colors sprinkled on the top of the solution in your trough, then take it carefully off, and hang it up to dry. To produce a variety of patterns with changes of colors: When your gum-water or solution is in the trough, first throw on red till it is nearly covered, then yellow or black and green also, you may add a little purple, with plenty of gall and water in it. To form different patterns, use an instrument similar to a rake's head or a comb, twelve or eighteen inches in length, stirring the colors with the teeth, in circular or zig-zag, oval, or any other direction your taste may suggest. For another:

Use the same colors as before, with the addition of blue in oil of turpentine. Another: Begin by throwing on yellow, then red, black, and green; draw lines through the colors with your comb, and afterwards throw on blue, pink, green, or purple, thinned with gall and oil of turpentine. Another, handsome pattern: Throw in fine red for veins, then blue, in oil of turpentine. Another: Throw on some dark blue, mixed with oil of turpentine. Prepare your paper first for this color, stained with French berries boiled in water, add a little spirit of liquid blue, then carefully brush it over the paper. To obtain variety, you may stain your paper first with red, pink, yellow, or blue, before dipping. Another: Use yellow ochre, burnt red, and Venetian red, of equal parts, orange orpiment, or rose pink. Another: Orange brown, two parts of Venetian red, and one part of orange lead. Another: Umber color, equal parts of orange lead, Venetian red, and ivory black. To lighten the color use more orange lead; to darken it, more black. Another: Cinnamon color, a little Prussian blue and Venetian red. For fine work in splendid colors, use drop lake, vermilion, one part, rose pink, three or four parts mixed together, indigo, Prussian blue, king's yellow, or pink, &c.

For marbling paper, a trough of the following description is required, made of wood: About two inches in depth, the length and breadth being half an inch larger than the sheets of paper, the sides must be sloped off to give the required width at the top, and to prevent waste of color; the outside edges must be leveled off to prevent any drops of color which may fall on them from flowing back into it and soiling its contents. Fill the trough with the following solution : Take of gum tragacanth a quarter of a pound, soak it three days in a gallon of water, after this dilute it to the thickness of gum used in miniature painting, strain it through a hair-sieve on cloth, and pour it into the trough. When you use this solution stir it well in the trough. A skimmer or clearing stick must be provided for each trough, two or three inches wide, half an inch thick, and as long as the inside of the trough, for the purpose of clearing the surface of filth. As many glazed pipkins as you have colors will be required to keep them separately. When ground very fine in water to the thickness of paste, and thinned down with equal quantities of ox-gall and oil of turpentine. Spreading-brushes have been used for the purpose of throwing the colors on the solution, but the patent tin-case circular-brush is far better for the purpose, as a cistern at the back supplies the brush with the color, effecting a saving, the machine being held over the trough with the left hand, and working with the right. To produce spots like lace-work, supply your circular-brush sparingly with the colors thinned with water; and in doing this, if the spots spread out too large, the colors have too much gall; if, after spreading, they contract again, there is too little gall. To remedy the former case, add more color; the latter, more gall. Your paper for marbling should be prepared by dipping in water over night, the sheets laid on each other with a weight on them. The process is as follows : The whole surface of the solution must be covered with the various colors for the purpose, then, with an instrument like a large comb, termed in the trade quills, stir the surface in whirls, streaks, &c., according to the pattern you wish to produce, proceed now to lay on in the most gentle and even manner your sheets of paper upon the colors in the trough, the parts which do not touch the color softly press with the hand; take them off with care and hang them up to dry upon round rods, about an inch and a half in diameter. When the solution of gum in the trough gets dirty, throw it away, and supply its place with some fresh; and when the colors become too thick for use in the pots, add fresh color ground with water, and a little gall added, and well stirred together; be particular in getting good oil of turpentine, and keeping your colors clean. Observe, for book edges, dip one volume at a time, doing the ends first. It is the safest way to tie the book between boards before dipping. For convenience and economy a small trough may be used for books. Marbled paper is glazed by a machine. Book edges are polished by the agate burnisher. Hot-pressing may be used for any fancy-work. Paper-varnish will beautify the paper; paste and moisture takes the glaze off marbled paper.

For graining on paper, mix the color you intend for the ground in London-size, or parchment-size; with a wide brush put your color on quickly for the ground. Black, red, and white, or any color you may choose, have ready prepared in size, throw on the spots while the ground is wet. Use the patent circular-brush graniting machines* to throw in the spots, and immediately after sift on your glass, frost, or smalts, and put aside for drying.

To prepare the Ground for the Oak Rollers.—Stain your white lead with raw terradasienna and red lead, or with chrome yellow and Venetian red; thin it with oil and turps, and strain it for use. When the ground-work is dry, grind in beer Vandyke brown, whiting, and a little burnt terradasienna, for the graining-color; or you may use raw terradasienna with a little whiting, umbers, &c.

Oil for Graining Oak.—Grind Vandyke brown in turps, add as much gold-size as will set it, and as much soft soap as will make it stand the comb.

Should it set too quickly, add a little boiled oil. Put a teaspoonful of gold-size to half a pint of turps, and as much soap as will lay on a twenty-five cent piece; then take a little soda mixed with water and take out the veins.

Spirit Graining for Oak.—Two pounds of whiting, quarter of a pound of gold-size, thinned down with spirits of turpentine; then tinge your whiting with Vandyke brown and raw terradasienna ground fine, strike out your lights with a fitch dipped in turpentine, tinged with a little color to show the track, and every few strokes wipe off the color to show the lights. If your lights do

---

* These machines are in use to a considerable extent in England, but not much, that I am aware of, in this country.

not appear clear, add a little more turpentine. Turpentine varnish is a good substitute for the above mentioned.

This kind of graining must be brushed over with beer, with a clean brush, before varnishing. Strong beer must be used for glazing up top graining or shading.

Another Cream. — Mix raw terradasienna, red and white lead, to the tint required for the ground: when this is applied and dry and made smooth with fine glasspaper, the graining color may be applied, for which take four ounces of sugar of lead, four ounces of raw terradasienna, whiting, and Vandyke brown, and grind them quite stiff in boiled linseed oil. Take eight ounces of bee's wax and melt it in an iron ladle or earthen pipkin, and when fluid take it a distance from the fire, and pour in gradually spirits of turpentine, to the consistency of thick treacle: put a small quantity of this (grainer's cream) into the graining color, in order to keep it from flowing together. If the composition should set too quick before it can be conveniently worked, add a small portion of boiled oil; or, should it flow too freely, add some of the cream. This style of oak requires working with combs of various sizes. Observe, that for the purpose of graining mouldings, it will be necessary to prepare small combs in a variety of forms.

Application.—Spread the graining color over the sur face of the work with a large paint-brush, about half worn; take a coarse comb and pass over it in a straight direction, pressing moderately hard; after which, take a finer comb and pass over it several times in a wavy direction; then with an ivory-comb, with the two outside teeth broken off, pass over the centre of the work with a very tremulous motion of the hand, in order to produce the finest grain which is in the centre of the tree. To produce flowers or veins, use a piece of thin wash-leather, wrapped tight round the thumb, and wipe them out with the thumb nail, or twist the leather to a point and hold it between the thumb and finger. By taking these methods, the thickest or finest veins may be struck out successfully. When the whole of your work is dry, dip the flat hog's hair graining-brush into a small quantity of burnt umber, ground up in ale very thin, and pass over it in a straight direction. This will leave the fine transparent grain so natural to this wood. When dry, varnish.

Another Oak.—This ground-color is prepared with white lead and chrome yellow, heightened with a little Venetian red. When your ground is dry, take burnt umber and grind it in equal parts of boiled oil and turpentine; when this is done, take an equal proportion of copperas (white vitriol), previously baked in an oven or stove, till the moisture is evaporated, which will take place in a few minutes. This operation must be performed in a glazed earthen bowl, as it will adhere so firmly to any rough vessel that it would be difficult to separate them. When the copperas is burnt, it must be ground in raw linseed oil, and mixed with the above ingredients; then take one-sixth in bulk of castile soap, melted over the fire in a little boiled oil; mix this also with the other ingredients; thin the whole down with boiled oil and turpentine to the proper consistency for graining. If the grain should run together too freely, use a greater proportion of spirits of turpentine; or should it set too quick, add more boiled oil. Proceed to finish exactly as in the last.

To Imitate Oak in Distemper.—To prepare the ground for this, make a very light yellow with stone ochre and white lead. The graining colors used for this specimen are equal quantities of raw umber and stone yellow, ground very fine in ale. This should be kept in a well-corked bottle, in order to keep dust and other impurities from it; and when required for use, it should be diluted with ale to a proper consistency for graining. When your ground is dry, take a large tool well filled with this color, rub it over the panel in an even manner, have ready a sponge, a bowl of water, and a straight edge. Place the straight edge against the work, and, with the sponge moistened with water, draw out the light shades in a perpendicular manner, then wipe with a brush the panel, striking the work with the end of the brush in quick succession till you get to the bottom, when, if done according to these directions, it will leave the natural grain of the wood. When this operation is finished, immediately take a piece of wash-leather, moistened, and wipe out the veins; and when this is dry, put in some dark veins of the same color; allow this to dry also, then, with a flat hog's hair brush, dipped into burnt umber thinly diluted with ale, pass over the panel in a perpendicular direction; and as soon as one panel is finished, take a wet rag or sponge and carefully wipe off all the color which may have gone beyond the panel. When all your panels are finished, commence on the middle upright styles, varying the grain according to taste, but always in a downward direction. When all the middle styles are thus far completed, lay the straight edge over the work finished, and pass the tool with a little of the graining color from top to bottom of the door; this will make a neat job, both at the end of the styles and panels. When dry, take the flat graining-brush and dip it in the thin glaze of umber, and pass over the work, not too straight and formal, but in a spirited manner, occasionally giving a free turn to the brush, which will give a pleasing variety and make the imitation look quite natural. When dry, varnish.

N. B.—All distemper-graining requires two good coats of varnish: beer it over before you varnish it a second time.

Another Oak.—This method of imitating oak in distemper is so excellent, that should it be exposed continually to the hot rays of the sun, it will never fade. Make a rich ground-color with stone ochre, burnt terradasienna, chrome yellow, and white lead. For your graining-color, dissolve some gum Arabic in hot water, and mix it with raw terradasienna, whiting, and Vandyke, ground in beer. When the ground is dry, spread the surface very even, then take a dry duster and draw it down upon the work, pressing moderately hard; comb the color while wet, and allow it to get perfectly dry, then with a camel-hair pencil, dipped in clear water, put in your veins. Allow the work to remain a few seconds till the water has dissolved the gum Arabic, and then beat the veins out with a dry duster or cloth, in a downward direction. After this, use the flat brush, and pass over the work with a thin glaze of Turkey umber, ground in ale. Should the veins not beat out sufficiently clear, add a little more gum to the color, but care must be taken not to put too much, as the work would be likely to crack. When dry, varnish.

To Imitate Old Oak.—To make an exceedingly rich color for the imitation of old oak. The ground is a composition of stone ochre or orange chrome and burnt terradasienna. The graining-color is burnt umber or Vandyke brown, to darken it a little. Observe that the above colors must be used whether the imitation is in oil or distemper. When dry, varnish.

To Grain Oak in Distemper.—The ground either light or dark. When the ground is dry and made quite smooth, then with a fitch form your veins with a little ochre, ground in turpentine varnish. When the distemper-color for the combining is applied after the veins are formed on the plain ground, then whip and comb in with your color mixed with beer. When dry, varnish; which varnish will bring the lights out which were first struck out. When dry, wet the whole with a little beer, glaze up and varnish.

To Imitate Old Oak in Oil.—Grind Vandyke and whiting in turpentine, add a bit of common soap to make it stand the comb, and thin it with boiled oil.

Pollard Oak in Distemper, with a Roller or handwork.—Form large dark patches with Vandyke brown on the ground; then with a softener draw from patch to patch, then take a short cut hair pencil or a small piece of sponge tied to the end of a stick, and by turning it round between the thumb and finger, form your curls or knots on the patches: to render it more showy, put in some patches of lake and burnt terradasienna, and form knots in the same way as above; then top grain, which grain must cross all the other grains. As soon as dry, which will be in a few minutes, give it a coat of equal parts of gold-size and turps, to be used as a varnish, as it dries quickly where expedition is required. When dry, glaze over with Vandyke brown or ivory-black, ground in beer, then with a soft piece of rag or sponge take out your shades, soften, varnish, and finish your work.

To Imitate Pollard Oak.—The ground-color is prepared with a mixture of chrome yellow, vermilion, and white lead, to a rich, light buff. The graining-colors are Vandyke brown and small portions of raw and burnt terradasienna and lake, ground in ale or beer. Fill a large tool with color, spread even the surface to be

7

grained, and soften with the badger-hair brush. Take a moistened sponge between the thumb and finger, and dapple round and round in kind of knobs, then soften very lightly; then draw a softener from one set of knobs to the other while wet, to form a multiplicity of grains, and finish the knots with a hair-pencil, in some places in thicker clusters than others. When dry, put the top grain on in a variety of directions, and varnish with turps and gold-size; then glaze up with Vandyke and strong ale. To finish, varnish with copal.

Pollard Oak in Oil.—The ground is a rich buff, prepared the same as the pollard oak in distemper. The graining-colors are: equal portions of burnt Turkey umber or Vandyke, raw terradasienna and burnt copperas, ground separately in boiled oil or turps very stiff; then mix them together, and thin the whole with spirits of turpentine; then with a large sash-tool rub a very light coat on the panel, and, while wet, take the flat graining brush, containing a very thin row of hairs, dip it into the color, and in a spirited manner dapple in various directions, then dip the brush into the burnt umber, which has been made quite thin with spirits of turpentine, and throw on some very fine spirits. When the colors are set, take the same flat brush, dip it into a thin glaze of burnt umber, and put the grain on in a curly direction. Care must be taken to have a sufficient quantity of oil in the colors to bind them, and to finish but a small part of the surface at once, in order to keep it moist, the work will then blend itself.

A good Ground for Mahogany.—One pound of the best English Venetian red, two ounces of chrome yellow, ground together in equal portions of linseed oil and turpentine. If a light ground is required, use the same quantities of red lead and chrome yellow; a little vermilion will increase the richness of the color. Use for the graining-color equal quantities of Vandyke brown and burnt terradasienna, ground in ale or beer, well ground on a clean stone; a small piece of lake may be added for the light grain. The feather is formed with a graining-roller in a few seconds, ready for softening.

To Imitate Mottled Mahogany.—The ground is prepared with the best English Venetian red, red lead, and a small portion of white lead. The graining-colors required are burnt terradasienna ground in ale, with a small portion of Vandyke brown, sufficient to take away the fiery appearance of the terradasienna. Cover the surface to be grained, soften with the badger's-hair brush, and while wet take a mottling-roller, and go over the lights a second time, in order to give a variety of shade; then blend the whole of the work with the badger softener. Put the top grain on with the same color; when dry, varnish.

Another.—This ground is prepared with vermilion and a very small portion of white lead and chrome yellow. The graining-color is Vandyke brown and a little crimson lake, ground up in ale. After the ground is dry and made smooth, spread a thick coat on the surface to be grained, and soften with the badger hair-brush; take out the lights on each side, and use a roller with the imitation carved on leather, wetted with water; it is expeditious in forming a feather, or mottling. Blend the whole together with the badger hair-brush till the work appears very soft. Top grain, and the effect will be beautiful. When dry, varnish.

To Imitate New Mahogany.—This is an excellent method of preparing for the imitation of new mahogany. The ground-color must be prepared with equal quantities of chrome yellow and red lead, with a little burnt terradasienna. The graining-color is prepared with equal portions of raw and burnt terradasienna, finely ground in ale or beer. After the ground is dry, spread a thick coat on the panel, then work with a mottler and softener. When dry, put on the top grain with burnt terradasienna. Varnish when dry.

Another.—This ground is prepared with stone ochre, red lead, and a small quantity of burnt terradasienna. The graining-color is a mixture of Vandyke brown and dragon's blood: for the top grain a greater proportion of Vandyke brown must be used. Varnish as before.

To Imitate Rosewood with Rollers.— Brush on the graining-color as even as you can; then pass the graining-rollers over to form the hearts and knots, &c. Previous to doing this, let the rollers be wetted with water and rolled on a cloth. When the work is dry, brush it over with a thin coat of gold-size and turps: when this is dry, top grain again with rollers, and varnish it over.

For the ground-color, mix the best English Venetian red with linseed oil and turps, to which add a little patent dryers. Vermilion will form a superior ground, but is more expensive.

Another.—Mix vermilion and a small quantity of white lead for the ground. Take rose pink, tinged with a little lamp-black, or Vandyke brown, and grind very fine in oil, then take a flat graining-brush, with the hairs cut away at unequal distances, and put on the grain as if wending round a knot. When nearly dry, take a graining-comb that is used for oak, and draw down the grain. This will give it the appearance of nature. When dry, varnish.

Another.—The ground is a bright red, prepared exactly the same. For the graining-colors, grind separately some burnt terradasienna and ivory-black, very fine in ale; mix them together, and with the tool well cover the surface of the work, then wipe it with the softener, to form the small speckled grain. When dry, take a small flat graining-brush, well filled with ivory-black, and put on the top grain in a knotty form; after this, cut the top grain asunder by putting in the heavy hearts with rollers. When the first coat of varnish is dry, grind a small quantity of lake in ale, and with a camel-hair pencil touch round the knots and other parts of the work. When dry, finish with a coat of clear varnish.

Another.—This ground-color is prepared with vermilion and small quantities of white lead and crimson lake. When the ground is dry and made very smooth, take Vandyke brown, ground in oil, with a small tool spread the color over the surface in different directions, forming kind of knots. Before the work is dry, take a piece of leather, and with great freedom strike out the light veins; having previously prepared the darkest tint of Vandyke brown, or gum asphaltum, immediately take the flat graining-brush, with few hairs in it, draw the grain over the work and soften. When varnished, the imitation will be excellent.

Another, in Size.—Mix Venetian red, white lead powder, vermilion, and common size, the consistency of which, when cold, must be of a weak, trembling jelly. With this composition paint the work twice over. When the ground is dry, take some lamp-black, finely ground in beer, and beat the white of an egg into it; take the flat graining-brush, dipped in the black, and put on the grain.

When dry, stain the first coat of varnish with rose pink, finely ground in turpentine, and finish the work by giving it a coat of clear varnish.

To Imitate Bird's-eye Maple.—The ground is a light buff, prepared with white lead, chrome yellow, and a little vermilion, or English Venetian red, to take off the rawness of the yellow. The graining-color is equal parts of raw umber and terradasienna, ground in ale to the proper consistency. Spread the surface of the work with this color, and, having some of the same prepared a little thicker, immediately take a sash-tool or sponge, and put on the dark shades, and soften with the badger hair-brush ; before the color is dry, put on the eyes by dabbing the dotting machine on the work. When dry, put on the grain with the camel's-hair pencil in the prominent parts, to imitate the small hearts of the wood. When dry, varnish.

Another.—The ground for this, prepare in oil, with white lead, turps, and stained with chrome or stone ochre, and a little red. The graining-colors are three parts of raw umber, and one of raw terradasienna, ground fine in ale. Make part of this color quite thin, and rub a transparent coat over the work, and while wet take the flat hog's-hair graining-brush and dip it into some thicker color, draw the veins very much curled, and rather inclining downwards ; then take a feather or goose-quill, and with it pass over the work in the same direction as the flat-brush was used, occasionally giving a sharp turn, and, if necessary, pass over the work again ; this will split them into a variety of forms. While wet, soften the whole together, and put in the eyes by dabbing the points of the fingers or rollers, &c., on the work, and occasionally using the hair-pencil. When the whole of the work is dry, top grain with a thin glaze of raw umber, finely ground in ale : when dry, varnish.

To Imitate Curled Maple.—Prepare a light yellow for the ground, by mixing chrome yellow and white lead, tinged with Venetian red. The graining-color is a mixture of equal portions of raw terradasienna and Vandyke, ground in ale. Spread the surface to be grained in an even manner, then with a piece of cork rub across the work to and fro, to form the grains which run across the wood; soften, and when dry, lightly top grain with the same color: when dry, varnish.

Another Maple.—The ground is prepared precisely the same. The graining-colors are equal quantities of raw and burnt terradasienna, ground in water, and diluted with ale. Fill a tool with the color, and spread the surface even; then take a long piece of stout buff leather, cut to a straight edge, and by holding it at each end, press the edge hard against the work, draw the leather down, and it will leave the lights and shades; or use a patent roller to take out the lights, which is very expeditious in its operation; when softened, top grain, and varnish when dry.

Another.—Put on the color with a tool; then with a sponge mottle and soften; then put in small eyes with your roller or fingers on the mottle; then put on the fine top grain with a fine pencil, forming the heart of the wood, and shade underneath with a bit of buff leather.

Curled Maple, in Oil, for Outside Work.—Prepare a rich ground, by mixing chrome yellow, white lead, and burnt terradasienna. For the graining-color, grind equal parts of raw terradasienna and umber with a little burnt copperas in turpentine, and mix with it a small quantity of grainer's-cream. Thin the color with boiled oil, then fill a tool and spread the surface even, and rub out the lights with the sharp edge of a piece of buff leather, which must now and then be wiped to keep it clean; soften the edges of the work very lightly, and when dry, put on the top grain with burnt umber and raw terradasienna, ground in ale, with the white of an egg beat into it; when dry, varnish.

Satinwood.—This ground is prepared with white lead, stone ochre, and small quantities of chrome yellow and burnt terradasienna. The graining-color is one-third of raw terradasienna and whiting, ground in pale ale very thin; then spread the color over the surface to be grained. While wet, soften, and have ready a wet roller or mottling-brush, in order to take out the lights; blend the whole with the badger hair-brush. When the work is dry, take the flat-brush, and, with the same color, put on the top grain: when dry, varnish.

Another.—Prepare the ground for this the same. The graining-colors are equal quantities of raw terradasienna and raw umber, with a little burnt terradasienna, and a very small portion of whiting, ground in ale or beer. Spread the color even over the surface of the work, and soften, then take the roller which has the feather carved on it. Soften, and when dry top grain with the same color. Varnish as before.

Another.—The ground make with white lead, chrome yellow, and a little vermilion, till a very light cream color is produced. Well cleanse the work from dust and grease, take a little of the best stone yellow, and a very small portion of burnt terradasienna and whiting, ground in pale ale, and cover with a thin coat the surface to be grained. Take a piece of wetted sponge and dab it on various parts of the work, and a roller, in order to take out the lights. As soon as you have produced as much dapple as required, soften the whole of the work. When dry, put on the top grain with a thin glaze of the same color, thinned with beer: when dry, varnish.

To Imitate Yew Tree.—The ground is a reddish buff. For the graining-color, grind in ale equal portions of Vandyke brown and burnt terradasienna, with a small quantity of raw terradasienna. When the ground is dry, spread the surface even with the color, and soften; then with a piece of cork with a sharp edge, rub the work cross and cross, in order to form the fine grain as in curled maple, and soften the same way of the grain. When dry, dip the tip of your fingers in the graining-color to form the eyes or knots, and put in the small touches with the camel-hair pencil. When dry, put on the top grain, and when this is dry, varnish.

To Imitate Hair-Wood.—For the ground-color, take white lead and thin it with turpentine, and slightly stain it with equal quantities of Prussian blue and lamp-black. For the graining-color, grind in ale a mixture of Prussian blue and raw terradasienna; when the ground is dry, spread a transparent coat of the graining-color on the surface of the work, and soften; then with the cork, mottle by rubbing it to and fro across the work to form the fine, long grain or mottle. When this is done, soften and top grain in a wavy but perpendicular direction: varnish when dry.

Hair-Wood for Chairs.—Paint the chair a light gray, by adding a little Prussian blue with white lead, ground very stiff in boiled linseed oil, and thinned down with turps to the consistency required. When this is dry, take some of the ground-color, made considerably thinner with turpentine, and with a common paint-brush put a very light coat on a small part of the work at once, as the grain must be laid on before the last coat sets, otherwise the colors will not blend together: having provided some thicker color, made darker by adding more Prussian blue, take a feather, or short gilder's-tip, dip it into the color, and put on the fine, long vein cross ways, similar to the grain of curled maple. When the work is thus far finished, take a small flat graining-brush, and put on the top grain with the same color; when the whole of the work is ornamented and quite dry, it may be completed with two coats of colorless copal varnish.

N. B.—If a green color is desired, substitute mineral green for Prussian blue, both for the ground and graining-colors.

To Imitate Oriental Verd-antique marble.—Mix the ground black in oil-paint, and made quite smooth. For the graining-color, take white lead in oil, and made quite fluid in spirits of turpentine. This, laid on with a common sash-tool, in broad, transparent veins. so thin in places that the white is scarcely perceptible, and in other places nearly opaque. While the white is wet, take a piece of wash-leather, and dab it on in different parts of the work, leaving it in the form of shells or other fossil remains. While the color is still wet, take a square piece of cork, and, notching it in two or three places, turn it round on the work between the thumb and finger. This will leave the circles more natural than pencil: when this is done, cut away part of a feather at unequal distances, pass this once over the white to take out irregular veins on the black ground, and by suddenly checking the hand, make it take an angular direction. When the work is sufficiently veined, let it remain till it gets dry before more can be done to it; when dry, it must be glazed over in distemper colors, in some places with raw terradasienna, in others, Prussian blue; and some parts must be left black and white. When the work is dry, take a feather and dip it into whiting ground fine in milk, and with it draw the fine veins over the work; a few fine lines with a camel-hair pencil may also be made to curl over the light parts with Prussian blue. When dry, it will be ready for the last glaze, which make of raw terradasienna and a small portion of Prussian blue, mixed together in equal parts of boiled oil and turpentine. This will give the whole of the work the appearance of a beautiful green: when dry, varnish.

Observe that verdantique, Egyptian, and Serpentine, are the three principal marble greens, and most varied in their colors; but those with all other greens may be produced in a similar manner to the verdantique; but it will be advisable for the learner to procure some specimens of the different kinds of green marbles before he attempts to imitate what he has never seen.

To Imitate Black and Gold Marble.—This description of marble is now in great use. The ground is a deep jet black, or a dead color in gold size, drop black and turps; second coat, black japan, commence veining; mix white and yellow ochre with a small quantity of vermilion to give a gold tinge: dip the pencil in this color, and dab on the ground with great freedom some large patches, from which small threads must be drawn in various directions. In the deepest parts of the black a white vein is sometimes seen running with a great number of small threads attached to it; but care must be taken that these threads are connected with, and run in some degree in the same direction with the thicker veins. If durability is not an object, and the work is required in a short time, it may be executed very quick in distemper colors, and when varnished it will look well.

Dove Marble.—The ground is a lead color. If the work is new, it will be necessary to give it two very thin coats of ground-color, which must be made to dry hard, taking care to rub it smooth with fine glass-paper after each coat, and not to rub the color off the sharp edges of the wood: it must now remain till quite hard. For the graining, take some of the lead color, such as used for the ground, and make it quite thin with turpentine, and rub a light coat over a small part of the work, with some dryers in to give a drying quality, and make it thin with spirits of turpentine; then take a small graniting-machine, with a whitish color, to form the small specks or other fossil remains: proceed in the same way till the whole surface is covered, taking the precaution to paint but a small part of the ground at once, that the colors may have sufficient time to blend together while wet, otherwise the work will appear harsh. When these colors are set, take some of the thin ground-color, and, with a fitch or small sash-tool, put in the faint, broad veins; then take a camel-hair pencil and put in a multiplicity of very fine veins over the whole surface of the work, crossing each other in every direction. When this is done, make the color a few shades lighter, by adding white lead, and with a feather dipped in the color, pass over the broad veins in the same direction, forming streams or threads. When this is done, take some thin white, and, with a camel-hair pencil, go partly over the same vein with short, thick touches; then with a fine stripping-pencil, and with the same color, pass over the work, forming very fine lines, crossing each other in an angular direction. When the work is hard, rub it smooth with very fine glass-paper, and finish by putting on a coat of colorless varnish.

Observe that the first layer of veins must be exceedingly faint, so much so that they are scarcely perceptible, as the lighter shades are put on, the former veins will appear sunk from the surface of the work to the depth of several inches, which will give an admirable effect for chimney-pieces, table-tops, wash-stands, &c., where the work is exposed to close inspection.

Another.—The ground is a light lead color, and when perfectly dry, take a small paint-brush and scumble on irregular broad veins of white and black. Soften with a dry duster, and when sufficiently blended, the color must form light and dark shades, and not a decided black or white. This style of graining is well calculated for large columns, halls, and all outside work, as it has a strikingly bold and heavy appearance. A few veins may be added with advantage.

Another.—The ground the same as the last. The graining-colors are lamp-black and a little Prussian blue, ground together very stiff in turps and a little white vitriol, to act as a dryer, and thinned with boiled oil. Mix small portions of these colors together with white lead, making the mixture a very little lighter than the ground-color, and with a fitch put on the broad veins; then fill a camel-hair pencil and go over the same veins again with a lighter color: when this is done, go partly over the same vein again with white, slightly tinged with blue-black, and made very thin with turpentine; a few white veins may be made to run over the surface of the work in various directions, being careful not to make them too prominent.

White-Veined Marble.—This ground is a pure white. For the graining-color, white lead ground stiff in raw oil, and made very thin with turpentine; then with a paint-brush rub a light coat on a small part of the surface; then with a fitch scumble over the work with broad, faint veins of white, heightened with a little Prussian blue and lamp-black, and with a camel-hair pencil go over the work in various directions, forming the fine angular lines; then with a little darker color go over the broad veins rather sparingly: when this is done, make the color still darker, and with a fine pencil or feather go over the same veins, forming very small threads intersecting each other and running to a centre, and then suddenly striking out again in all directions. A good effect may be given by passing a few fine dark veins across different parts of the work in an opposite direction to the veins already laid on. When the work is dry, use colorless varnish.

Sienna Marble.—The ground is stone yellow or raw sienna. When the ground is dry, mix some stone yellow with white lead, have ready some white paint, and with these two colors, used separately, put in some broad transparent shades of white and yellow, and while wet, blend them together with a soft duster. Take some Venetian red and a little Prussian blue mixed with it, and with a hair-pencil put in some broad veins in the same direction as the shades run; then for the darker veins take a mixture of Venetian red, lake, and Prussian blue, and with a feather draw them over the first layer of veins in fine threads, running to a centre, and then striking out again in fine transparent veins in different directions. When this is done, mix Prussian blue and lake together, and with a fine pencil put in the darkest and finest veins over those previously laid on. Put in a few dark touches of burnt terradasienna between the fine veins, which are formed into small masses. If the first shades are not sufficiently varied, a thin and separate glaze of burnt and raw terradasienna may be applied in different parts of the work. All the above graining-colors should be ground in spirits of turpentine and gold-size sufficient to bind them.

Italian Marble.—This looks bold, and is well adapted for columns, &c., and is easy to imitate. The ground, a light buff. For the graining-colors, prepare a rich, warm buff, made in the following manner : Mix stiff in boiled oil, white lead, and good stone ochre, and tinge with vermilion ; then grind some burnt terradasienna very fine in boiled oil, and put it into another pot : mix some pure white stiff in oil, and keep this separate. Thin these colors with turpentine : have ready a brush for the buff, and another for the terradasienna. Proceed to work as follows : Take the brush intended for the buff moderately full of color, and dab it on freely and carefully in different patches, some of them larger than others, and varying them as much as possible.

When, these are laid on, take the other brush and fill in with the terradasienna the spaces between ; as soon as this is done, take a dry duster or softener, and blend the edges together, making it appear as soft as possible. Proceed in this manner till the whole is finished ; then take a hair-pencil and draw a few thin white veins over the work, varying them as much as necessary : take another pencil for the terradasienna, and run a few lines intermixing with the whole. Varnish when dry.

Red Marble.—For the ground, put on a white tinged with lake or vermilion; then apply deep rich reds in patches, filling up the intermediate spaces with brown and white mixed in oil; then blend them together: if in quick drying colors, use about half turps and gold-size. When dry, varnish; and while the varnish is wet, put in a multitude of fine white threads, crossing the whole work in all directions, as the wet varnish brings the pencil to a fine point.

Jasper Marble.—Put on a white ground lightly tinged with blue; then put on patches of rich reds or rose pink, leaving spaces of the white ground; then partly cover those spaces with various browns to form fossils, in places running veins; then put in a few spots of white in the centre of some of the red patches, and leaving in places masses nearly all white. When dry, use the clearest varnish.

Blue and Gold Marble.—For the ground put on a light blue; then take blue, with a small piece of white lead and some dark common blue, and dab on the ground in patches, leaving portions of the ground to shine between; then blend the edges together with a duster or softener; afterwards draw on some white veins in every direction, leaving large open spaces to be filled up with a pale yellow or gold-paint; finish with some fine white running threads, a coat of varnish at last.

Imitation of Marbles in Distemper; White-Veined Marble.—This kind of marble has a splendid appearance on the walls of staircases, halls, bars of taverns, coffee-rooms, &c., and can be executed with great expedition. If the walls are broken and scaly, they must be well scraped and dusted, and two thin coats of lime white-wash applied. The second coat must be whiting mixed in milk, and at the same time have a little indigo, lamp-black, and Venetian red, ground separately in milk, which is sufficiently glutinous to bind the colors; have them all ready for use by putting each color into a separate bowl. A few long striping hair-pencils will be necessary, with long handles to them, in order to give more spirit and freedom to the work. When all the colors and tools are procured, commence by dividing the work into squares, about twenty inches by fourteen, to represent blocks of marble: this may be done by a long straight-edge and a black-lead pencil; the lines must be stout, in order to be seen through the last coat of whitewash. When the work is thus divided, commence at the top of the wall by putting on a very thin coat of whitewash, working downwards, taking the precaution to wet not more than one or two squares, as the whole of the work commenced upon must be blended with the dry duster, and finished before it gets dry. Immediately have ready in the bowl some whitewash slightly tinged with lamp-black and Venetian red, and with a large brush put in the broad faint vein, and blend it together with the brush used for the whitewash; then with a feather, or the flat graining-brush, containing a very thin row of hairs, draw the narrow veins in the same direction with the broad vein: take a large hair-pencil and put in some thick touches between the veins just laid on; immediately take some blue tinged with Venetian red, and made quite thin with milk, and with a fine camel-hair pencil put in a multiplicity of very fine veins, to represent, as it were, small streams of water running to a centre, and suddenly striking out in various directions, but always inclining the same way the broader veins run. When this is done, take a fine hair-pencil and put in a few fine white veins over the darkest shades. Have all the colors and tools in readiness before commencing work of this description, as it requires to be done with expedition. If the edges of the work should get too dry, they must be damped with milk, and so proceed till the wall is finished. The next thing to be done, is to draw the fine black lines with lamp-black, finely ground in size, in order to represent the small blocks, which may be easily executed with a pencil, such as is generally used for drawing the joints of brick-work, and with a beveled straight-edge. It should be observed, that the vein in each block should be made to run in a different direction, in order to distinguish one from another, and give the work a more natural appearance.

Italian Marble.—This kind of marble may be worked on walls. If a new wall, give it a coat of size worked in a jelly, in order to stop the suction of the wall. Mix a sufficient quantity of Indian red with strong beer, and put it into an earthen bowl; mix in beer whiting and French yellow, and tinge with English Venetian red till you produce a good buff. This you may know by trying it on a piece of paper and drying it by the fire, as it dries much lighter than it is while wet; then mix whiting with milk, as the beer would be apt to discolor it, or you may mix with size, and apply it warm. These colors must be mixed to the consistency of cream. Having the colors and brushes in readiness, proceed in the same manner as with oil colors, only instead of putting so many patches on the wall at once, you should dab on only eight or ten, and those very quick and freely; then fill up the spaces with the red, and blend the edges directly before the color sets, as it will be impossible to do anything with it after it dries. Proceed in the same manner till the whole of the wall is finished; put in the veins with distemper colors, as directed in oil colors.

Verd-antique.—This is an easy, and also a very excellent method of imitating this species of marble, and will be found very useful to the cabinet-maker, as it is well adapted for the tops of tables, side-boards, washstands, &c. It may be produced with good effect by any person, although he may not be accustomed to the art of painting. If the work is new, it may have one coat of dark lead color in oil paint, and when dry, it should be made smooth with fine glass-paper. Grind separately some white lead powder and lamp-black very fine in water and mixed with size. The black must be put on the work with a large sash-tool, leaving various narrow spaces in different parts of the work. When this is dry, the white lead must then be poured in thin streams on the black, and the table or wash-stand to be marbled is moved in various directions, taking the precaution to let the white fill up the small spaces which are left by the black. The floating must be repeated till the whole veins are sufficiently varied, and the small threads may be drawn from the wet masses of white over the dark parts by means of a feather. When the whole of the work is dry, the shells or fossil figures are dabbed carelessly on with a camel-hair pencil. When these colors are dry, have ready some raw terradasienna and Prussian blue, which has been finely ground in ale, and, with these colors used separately, put a thin glaze of each color on various parts of the work; allow this to dry also; then apply the green glaze, which is composed of raw terradasienna and Prussian blue, ground in spirits of turpentine, and mixed with copal varnish. When the work is varnished and polished, it will look well.

Another.—The ground is black, in oil paints, which well prepare and lay perfectly smooth on the surface of the work to be painted. It is necessary to give the work two thin coats, especially on mantle-pieces, fluted columns, pilasters, &c., in order that the sharp edges of the wood may be completely covered; and further observe, that in imitation of all fancy woods and marbles, particular care should be taken in laying on the ground-colors that the marks of the brush may not be visible; it will be better in all cases to give the surface to be grained two thin coats of ground-color. Take lampblack and put it into an iron kettle, place it over the fire till it gets red-hot, then take it from the fire and extinguish it on the slab. It must be stiffly ground in boiled oil, and thinned for use with spirits of turpentine: it will be necessary to add some burnt white vitriol, and a small quantity of litharge. When the ground is dry, commence graining by laying on white lead powder finely ground in water, and mixed with a small quantity of size, in order to bind and prevent its absorbing the varnish. The work must not be entirely covered with the white, but must be laid on in large streaks with a sash-tool, having previously prepared some lamp-black finely ground in size, with another sash-tool fill up the spaces which are left by the white, thereby covering the whole surface of the work; then with the badger-hair brush soften the whole of the work together while it is still wet, in order to make the veins run imperceptibly into each other. The whole of the work should be covered in this way at once; then take a large hair-pencil and dip it into the white, and on the darkest parts of the work dab the white carelessly, in spots of various sizes and forms, in order to represent the shells, &c. Take another pencil, dip it into the black, and go over the lightest parts of the work in the same manner. The flat graining-brush, containing a very thin row of hairs, may then be dipped into the white and drawn over the black, in order to form the small irregular veins. A dark blue vein may be made to run across the work; this should be put on in a wavy, zig-zag direction. When the work is perfectly dry, in order to give it the green shade, it must have a thin glaze of Prussian blue and raw terradasienna, the latter preponderating. The colors may be ground in spirits of turpentine, and mixed in copal varnish. When this is dry, the work may be finished by giving it another coat of varnish.

Marble to resemble Jasper.—The ground is mixed the same as for mahogany, with Venetian red, red lead, and a little chrome yellow, ground and thinned with equal parts of oil and turpentine: to increase the brilliancy of the color substitute vermilion or lake for the Venetian red; then throw on spots of white paint with a graining-machine while the ground is wet; blend them in with a softener or duster, and apply a little more white in the same manner. Blue, brown, or yellow, may be thrown in the same way, and blended altogether. When nearly dry, take a hair-pencil and form the large and small veins and threads: this latter part may be omitted or not, according to the taste of the workman.

N. B.—The above may be executed on a white ground and distemper colors applied with sash-tools and pencils, then varnished.

To Imitate Porphry Marble.—The ground is purple, brown, and rose pink. The graining-colors for this specimen are vermilion and white lead, ground separately in turpentine, and a little gold-size added to each color to bind them; but, as they cannot be ground sufficiently thin for use, more turpentine must be added to each color before it is applied. When the ground is quite dry, fill a large brush with vermilion, discharge nearly all the color by scraping the brush on the edge of a palette-knife, then holding a rod of iron in the left hand, strike the handle of the brush against it, letting the small red spots fall on the work till the surface is covered, or, what is much preferable to it, a patent graniting-machine, which will do the spotting much cleaner for all spotting purposes. Make the color a lighter shade by adding an equal quantity of white lead, and use it as before. Then with the clear, thin white, throw on the color the last time in very fine spots, and when dry, put in a few white veins across the work. When it gets quite hard, give it two coats of varnish. This kind of marble may be successfully imitated in distemper, which is preferable for inside work. The process is precisely the same as in oil; and as a substitute for gold-size and turpentine, take the white of a few eggs and beat them up in ale. By this method the work is executed with greater expedition, as it may be varnished at once. It is necessary, in the imitation of this marble, to procure some sheets of paper to place at the extent of the surface to be grained, in order to receive the superfluous spots.

Another.—This ground is red, and prepared with Venetian red, heightened with a little vermilion and white.

For the graining-color, add a little more white to the ground-color, and sprinkle the first layer on the same manner as in the last. When this coat is dry, the sprinkling may be repeated very sparingly, and in some parts more than others, with a mixture of Venetian red and vermilion. Sprinkle the last time with white in very fine spots. You may put an opaque white vein across the work running among the spots, from which transparent threads must be drawn in various directions; but this cannot be done till the whole of the work is quite dry and hard, when it may be performed with a sable pencil, and the threads drawn out with a feather. The work may then be varnished, and if due care be taken in sprinkling, the imitation will be excellent. Observe, that in the application of each color, a different circular-brush in the tin case, 2s. 6d. each, will be required.

To Imitate Granite.—For the ground-color, stain your white lead to a light lead color, with lamp-black and a little rose pink. Throw on black spots, with a graniting-machine, a pale red, and fill up with white a little before the ground is dry.

Another.—A black ground: when half dry, throw in vermilion, a deep yellow and white spots.

Another.—Oak, mahogany, and green grounds, look well with the same spots as used on other grounds.

To Polish Woods and Marbles.—Two and a half ounces of spirits of wine, one drachm of gum elemi, half an ounce of orange shellac. Pound the gums, and mix with the other ingredients.

To Imitate Black and Gold Marble, for table-tops, sideboards, &c.—The finest specimens of this marble are produced by spreading a leaf or two of gold in any part of the work where the gold veins are intended to run, and silver-leaf where the white vein is to be displayed. The black ground may then be painted rather thickly over the whole surface, covering the gold and silver leaves; and after the color has been on a short time, take a round-pointed bodkin, and draw the color in small reticulate veins from off the gold and silver-leaf; the metal will then show in fine lines. The larger masses may then be wiped off with leather. When the block is dry, the yellow and white veins may be painted as before directed, and drawn over the gold and silver-leaf, which will by this means show through them; and when the work is properly varnished and polished, it will give the appearance of nature. The colors may be ground in milk or strong beer, with the addition of a little size in the black.

To Imitate Tortoise Shell.—This beautiful color can be made in the following manner: Take of clear linseed oil twenty-four ounces; of Venice turpentine, or shellac, one ounce and a half; copal, of an amber color, six ounces; essence of turpentine, six ounces. The copal is to be placed in a matrass, and exposed to a moderate heat until it is liquefied; the linseed oil is then to be added in a boiling condition; then the Venice turpentine, or shellac, liquefied also; finally, in small portions, the spirits of turpentine. To be applied in the ordinary way.

Varnish for applying on Glass.—Take a quantity of powdered gum tragacanth, and dissolve it for thirty hours in the white of eggs, which should be well beat up; it is then gently to be rubbed on the glass with an ordinary brush.

Water Proof Polish.—This valuable article is made by putting one-fourth of an ounce of gum sandarac, one-fourth of an ounce of gum anime, and two ounces of gum benjamin, into a pint of spirits of wine, in a bottle tightly stopped. The bottle is to be placed either in a sand-bath or in hot water, till the gums are dissolved; the mixture must then be strained off; then shake it up with a quarter of a gill of the best clear poppy oil, and set it aside till needed.

To heighten the color of Gold or Brass.—If you wish to operate on yellow gold, dissolve in water one ounce of alum, six ounces of salt petre, two ounces of copperas, one ounce of white vitriol. If for red gold, take four ounces of melted yellow wax, two ounces and a half of red ochre in fine powder, one ounce and a half of calcined verdigris, half an ounce of calcined borax. Dissolve in water; apply with a soft cloth, and rub for a few minutes, and the surface will be very bright.

To dissolve Gold.—Take any given quantity platina or gold, dissolve it in *nitro-muriatic* acid, until no further effervescence will take place when heat is applied. The solution of gold or platina thus formed, must be evaporated to dryness by a gentle heat; by this means it will be freed from any excess of acid, which is quite requisite; then re-dissolve the dry mass in as little water as possible; next take an instrument, which is used by chemists for dropping liquid, known by the name of separating-funnel, having a pear-shaped body, tapering to a fine sharp point, and a neck capable of being stopped with the finger or a cork, which may contain a liquid ounce or more; this must be filled about one-fourth full with the liquid, and the other three parts must be with the best sulphuric ether. If this be properly managed, the liquids will not mix. Then place the tube in a horizontal position, and gently turn it round with the finger and thumb. The ether will very soon be impregnated with the gold or platina, which may be known by its changing its color; replace it in a perpendicular position, and let it stand at rest for twenty-four hours, having first stopped up the upper orifice with a cork.

The liquid will then be divided into two parts—the darkest coloring being underneath. To separate them, take out the cork and let the dark liquid flow out; when it has disappeared, stop the tube immediately with the cork, and what remains in the tube is fit for use, and may be called gilding-liquid. It should be put up in a bottle and corked tightly. The muriate of gold or platina, formed by digesting these metals in nitro-muriatic acid, must be entirely free from any excess of acid; for otherwise it will act too forcibly on the steel, and cause the coating of gold to peel off.

Pure gold must be employed. The ether must not be shaken with the muriate of gold, as advised in works of chemistry, for it will be sure then to contain acid; but if the two liquids be brought continually into contact by the motion described, the affinity between ether and gold is so strong as to overcome the obstacle of gravity, and it will hold the gold in solution. By gentle evaporation this etherial solution may be concentrated. The manner of using this solution of gold is well

INSTRUCTIONS FOR GILDING THE EDGES OF PAPER.

When you wish to gild the leaves of books, or fine letter paper, you must lay them in a horizontal position, and apply to the parts you wish to gild a composition made of two parts of candied sugar, and eight of Armenian bole, which are ground together to the proper consistence with water, and laid on by a brush with the white of an egg.

When nearly dry, this coating is to be smoothed by the aid of a burnisher. Then moisten the part with a sponge dipped in water and squeezed in the hand. After this the gold leaf must be taken up on a piece of cotton, and applied to the surface which has been moistened.

It is to be burnished by rubbing the burnisher over it several times from end to end. You must be careful not to wound the surface by the point. The burnishing must not take place until the part is dry.

General observations on the art of Gilding.—Instructions for executing it, &c., &c.

The gilding of leather is a beautiful process, and makes an excellent appearance if well executed. It is necessary that the leather should be first dusted over with very fine gum mastic or yellow resin. Then the stamps, or iron tools, are arranged on a rack before a clear fire, so as to be well heated, without becoming red-hot. If the tools are letters, they have an alphabetical arrangement on the rack. Each letter or stamp must be tried by imprinting its mark on the raw side of a piece of waste leather. By a little practice the workman will be able to judge of the heat. It is requisite that the tool should now be pressed downward on the gold-leaf, which will of course be indented and show the figure imprinted on it. Now the next stamp or letter is to be taken and stamped in like manner, and so on with the others, and taking care to keep the letters in an even line with each other, the same as those in a book.

The resin is melted by this operation, so the gold adheres to the leather. You can then wipe off the superfluous gold with a cloth, the gilded impressions remaining on the leather pretty permanently. You must slightly grease the cloth spoken of, to retain the gold wiped off, for if you do not, there may be quite a loss; the cloth thus will be completely saturated or loaded with gold. When this is the case, these cloths are generally sold to the refiner's, who burn them and recover the gold.

As regards the gilding of writings, drawings, and other things, on parchment or paper, but little need be said to enable the artist to execute them in good style. There are three ways of gilding them: one way is to mix a little size with the ink, and the letters are written as usual; when they are dry, a slight degree of stickiness is produced by breathing on them, upon which the gold-leaf is immediately applied, and by a little pressure may be made to adhere with sufficient firmness. Another method is to grind up some chalk or lead with strong size, and the letters are made with this by means of a brush. When the mixture is nearly dry, the gold-leaf may be laid on, and burnished afterwards. The best method is to mix some size with gold-powder, and form the letters of this with the brush used for such purposes.

In gilding steel, it is requisite that you pour some of the etherial solution of gold into a wine-glass, and dip into it the blade of a new knife, lancet, or razor; withdraw the instrument, and allow the ether to evaporate, the blade will then be found covered with a beautiful coat of gold. The blade may be moistened with a clean rag, or a small piece of dry sponge dipped into the ether, and the same effect will be produced. Figures of birds, females, trees, and various other things, may be put on the blade by first covering it with melted wax, letting it cool, and cutting the figures in the wax desired. The blade is then put into the solution of gold as before described.

If you desire to gild wood in oil, you must first cover or prime the wood with two or three good coatings of boiled linseed oil and carbonate of lead; and when dry, a thin coating of gold oil-size laid upon it. In twelve or fourteen hours, this sizing, if good, will be dry; then the gold-leaf may begin to be applied, dividing it and laying it on in the same way as in the case of water-gilding, with the difference that it is to be gently pressed down with a ball of soft cotton, when it will immediately adhere so firmly to the size, that after a few minutes the gentle application of a large camel's-hair brush will sweep away all the loose particles of the leaf without disturbing the rest. The advantages of this oil-gilding are, that it is quickly and easily done, it is durable, not easily injured by vicissitudes of weather, though exposed to the open air, and when soiled is readily cleaned by a little warm water and a soft brush. It is a little deficient in lustre, as it cannot be burnished.

Glass and porcelain can be vastly improved in beauty by gilding; to do which dissolve in boiled linseed oil an equal quantity either of copal or amber, and add as much oil of turpentine as will enable you to apply the compound or size thus formed, as thin as possible, to the parts of the glass intended to be gilt. The glass must be placed in a stove till it is so warm as almost to burn the fingers when handled. At this temperature the size becomes adhesive, and a piece of leaf-gold, applied in the usual way, will instantly stick. The superfluous portions of the leaf must be swept off, and when quite cold, it may be burnished, always taking care to interpose a piece of India paper between the gold and the burnisher.

Sometimes it takes place, that when the varnish is not very good, that by repeated washing the gold wears off; on this account the practice of burnishing it is sometimes resorted to. For this purpose, some gold powder is ground with borax, and in this state applied to the clean surface of the glass by a camel's-hair pencil; when quite dry, the glass is put into a stove, heated to about the temperature of an annealing-oven: the gum burns off, and the borax, by vitrifying, cements the gold with great firmness to the glass; after which it may be burnished. The gilding of porcelain is in like manner fixed by heat and the use of borax; and this kind of ware, being neither transparent nor liable to soften, and thus to be injured in its form in a low red heat, is free from the risk and injury which the finer and more fusible kinds of glass are apt to sustain from such treatment. Porcelain and other wares may be platinized, silvered, tinned, or bronzed, in a similar manner.

To gild copper, iron, brass, &c., you have to use mercury, with which the gold is amalgamated. The mercury is evaporated while the gold is fixed, by the application of heat; the whole is then burnished or left matte, in whole or in part, according as required. In the large way of gilding, the furnaces are so constructed that the volatilized mercury is again condensed and preserved for further use, so that there is no loss in the operation. There is also a contrivance by which the volatile particles of mercury are prevented from injuring the gilders.

There is a considerable difference between the gilding of wood and plaster, or marble with water-size. The principal difference, however, to be observed, when plaster or marble has to be gilt instead of wood, is to exclude the salt from the composition of the preparatory size, as in damp situations this would produce a white efflorescence upon the surface of the gold. Two coats of this size should be laid on; the first weak, that it may sink into the plaster or marble perfectly; the second must be strong, for obvious reasons.

When gilding carved wood with water-size, mix with the preparatory size a sufficient quantity of good glue, (which must be boiling-hot) and lay it upon the wood with a brush which has short bristles. Then apply six to ten coats, equal in quantity, of the white coating, and be careful that the projecting parts are well covered, as the beauty of the burnish on the gold depends greatly on this. It is necessary that the first coat should be laid on quite hot, dabbing it with the brush in such a manner that it may not be thicker in one place than another. The lower parts of the carving must be covered by dabbing it with a brush somewhat smaller. After putting on one coat of white, and previous to following it with a second, it is necessary the work should be examined, and if lumps are found in it, they must be reduced, and small hollows filled up by a cement made of whiting and glue worked together. Let the whole be now rubbed with a fish-skin, which will remove all manner of roughness.

The second, third, and remaining coats of white must have the size stronger than the first coat, but all of the same strength, otherwise a strong, superior coat will cause a weaker one under it to scale off: the operation of dabbing with the brush must be repeated in every successive coat, so as to unite the whole, that they may form a single, compact body. Each coat must also be perfectly dry before a new one is laid on. The whitened surface is now to be wet with the brush which has been used for putting on the whiting, dipped in fresh goldwater. Only a small portion should be wetted at a time, which should then be rubbed down with pumicestone, made flat for the parts which require to be of that form, and round and hollow, as may be required for the mouldings. Little sticks are used for clearing out those members of the mouldings which may have been filled up with whiting. The whitened parts are to be rubbed lightly, so as to make the surface smooth and even to the touch. At the same time, a brush which has become soft by using it with the whiting, is employed to clear out all the dust or dirt which has been found in the rubbing. The moisture is now to be dried up with a sponge, and any small grains which may remain, removed by the finger, a delicate and important operation.

The work is at last to be wiped with a piece of clean linen. Now the work must be returned to the carver, to have the fine and delicate cutting of the sculptured parts restored. A skilful workman will be able to reproduce on the whiting every characteristic trait which may have been obliterated.

Where bas-reliefs cast from moulds are laid on a flat or carved surface, instead of the wood itself being carved, as is very common at the present day, this repairing process will not be required. A moistened cloth is now to be passed over the parts that are to be matted or burnished, and a soft moistened brush over those which have been repaired. The whole is then to be washed with a soft sponge, and every speck and hair removed carefully. All the even parts should next be smoothed with rushes, taking care not to rub off the whiting. The coloring yellow is now to be applied very hot with a soft clean brush, so as to cover the whole work. This application must be lightly made, so as not to disturb the whiting.

The yellow tint serves to cover those deep recesses into which the gold cannot be made to enter; it serves also as a mordant for the gold-size. When this yellow covering becomes dry, the whole surface is to be again gently rubbed with rushes, to remove all specks or hairs which may be found on it, and to give a uniform surface without the slightest inequality. The gold-size, which is the next thing to apply, must be tempered by mixing it with some parchment-size that has been passed through a fine sieve. It is to be laid on warm with a small brush, the bristles of which are fine, long, and soft: there are brushes made expressly for this purpose. Three coats of the size will be sufficient. It is to be applied generally to the work, but you need not force it into the deeper parts. When the three coats of size are quite dry, the larger and smoother parts, which are intended to appear matted, are to be rubbed with a piece of new dry linen; this will cause the gold to extend itself evenly, and the water to flow over the sized surface without forming spots. To those parts which are not thus rubbed, but which are intended to be burnished, you must apply two additional coats of the same tempered gold-size, to which a little water has been added, to render it thinner.

The work being now ready for gilding, take a book of gold-leaf, place the leaves upon a cushion, cut them to the required size, and lay them on the work by means of hair-pencils of different sizes; first wetting the part, (and only that) on which the gold is to be applied with fresh and cool water. The deep recesses should be gilt before the more prominent ones. When the leaf is deposited in its place, water is applied, to make it spread easily, by means of a pencil behind it, but so as it may not flow, as this would occasion spots; it should also be breathed upon gently, and any waste water removed with the point of a pencil. Those parts of the gilding which it is wished to preserve of a matted appearance, should have a slight coat of parchment-size, which will prevent the gold from rubbing off.

The size should be warm, but not hot, and its strength

half as great as that used with the coloring yellow. The parts to which it is intended to give a more brilliant appearance, are burnished with a burnisher made of wolve's or dog's teeth or agate, mounted in iron or wooden handles, which must be kept dry throughout the process. The operation of burnishing is very simple. Take hold of the tool near to the tooth or stone, and lean very hard with it on those parts which are to be burnished, causing it to glide by a backward and forward movement, without once taking it off the piece.

When it is necessary that the hand should pass over a large surface at once, without losing its point of support on the work-bench, the workman, on taking hold of the burnisher, should place it just underneath his little finger; by this means the work is done quicker, and the tool is more solidly fixed in the hand. It will sometimes happen in gilding that small spots on the deeper parts are overlooked, or that the gold is removed in some parts in applying the matting-size. When this is the case, small pieces of gold-leaf are to be put on by means of a pencil, after moistening the deficient places with a small brush; when dry, each of these spots should be covered with a little size. When it is desired to give the work the appearance or "*moulu*," dip a small fine pencil into the vermilioning composition, and apply it delicately into the indentations, and such other parts where it will, by being reflected, give a good effect to the gold. To bind and finish the work well, a second coat of the matting-size should be passed over the matted parts, and hotter than the first by several degrees. What has been said in the foregoing pages on gilding, it is hoped will enable all to comprehend and apply it in practice.

MISCELLANEOUS.

A beautiful White Paint—For inside work, which ceases to smell, and dries in a few hours. Add one pound of frankincense to two quarts of spirits of turpentine; dissolve it over a clear fire, strain it, and bottle it for use; then add one pint of this mixture to four pints of bleached linseed oil, shake them well together, grind white lead in spirits of turpentine, and strain it; then add sufficient of the lead to make it proper for painting; if too thick in using, thin with turpentine, it being suitable for the best internal work on account of its superiority and expense.

For a pure White Paint.—Nut-oil is the best; if linseed oil is used, add one-third of turpentine.

To mix common White Paint.—Mix or grind white lead in linseed oil to the consistency of paste; add turpentine in the proportion of one quart to a gallon of oil; but these proportions must be varied according to circumstances. Remember to strain your color for the better sorts of work. If the work is exposed to the sun, use more turpentine for the ground-color to prevent its blistering.

For Knotting.—One pint of vegetable naptha, one teaspoonful of red lead, quarter of a pint of japaner's gold-size, seven ounces of orange shellac. Added together, set in a warm place to dissolve, and frequently shaken.

Another.—Mix white or red lead powder in strong glue-size, and apply it warm.

Common Flesh Color.—Stain your white lead with red lead, and mix with oil and turps.

Fine Flesh Color.—Is composed of white lead, lake and vermilion.

A beautiful Color for Carriages or Coaches, &c.—Mix Victoria lake with black japan.

A good Black for writing.—Vegetable black with boiled oil and turps.

Cream Color.—This is a mixture of chrome yellow, the best English Venetian red, white lead, and red lead, in oil.

Pearl Gray.—White lead, with equal portions of Prussian blue and lamp-black; mix with oil and turps.

Fawn Color.—Grind some burnt terradasienna very fine. Two or three pounds of this is sufficient to stain white lead for a large building.

N. B.—This color is of a superior shade, and very excellent for inside work.

Blue.—Grind Prussian blue in turps; other blue very fine in linseed oil, and mix it with white paint to the tint required.

Buff.—This is a mixture of French yellow and white lead, tinged with a little Venetian red, oil, and turps.

Straw.—A mixture of chrome yellow and white lead, oil, and turps.

Drab.—Raw umber and white lead, with a little Venetian red, linseed oil, and turps.

Another.—Burnt umber and white vitriol, with a little Venetian Red, oil, and turps, as before.

Steel.—Mix ceruse, Prussian blue, fine lac, and verdigris, in such proportions as to produce the required color.

Purple.—White lead, Prussian blue, and vermilion, with oil and turps.

Violet.—Is composed of vermilion, mixed with blue or black, and a little white.

French Gray.—White lead and Prussian blue, tinged with vermilion; and for the last coat substitute carmine or lake for the vermilion. Mix with oil and turps.

Silver.—Use white lead, indigo, and a small portion of black, as the shade may require.

Gold.—Mix Naples yellow or massicot with a small quantity of realgar and a little Spanish white.

Gold Paint.—Take one pound of spirits of wine, quarter of a pound of pure gum-lac, wash it till the water is no more red; when dry, grind it fine, and add it to the spirits of wine in a glazed earthen vessel of a size which will not be more than three-parts filled by the ingredients. Place this vessel in another which contains the water, after the manner of a glue-pot, over a fire without flame, keep it boiling till the gum is dissolved, and be careful that no lighted candle or flame come near it. Stir it while boiling with a piece of white wood. You may add a little turmeric-root or not at your own discretion. In case of its taking fire by accident, have a cloth ready in water to extinguish the flame. When dissolved, strain it through a strong linen cloth, bottle, and well cork it. To use this, paint over the wood three times with a soft brush; let each coat well dry before applying the other. If the work be silvered over first, it will resemble fine gold.

Dark Chesnut.—Mix red ochre and black. Use yellow ochre when you require to lighten the color, in oil.

Salmon.—White lead, tinged with the best English Venetian red, oil, and turps.

Peach Blossom.—White lead, tinged with orpiment; mixed with oil and turps.

Drab.—White lead with a little Prussian blue and French yellow, linseed oil, and turps.

Another.—White lead, with a little French yellow and lamp-black, linseed oil, and turps.

Another.—White lead, with a little chrome green.

Walnut Tree.—Mix ten ounces of white lead, five ounces of red ochre, with yellow ochre and umber, in quantities as required for darkening or lightening the shade. For the veining use ochre, umber, and black.

Chesnut, in Oil.—Mix red ochre and black; to make it lighter, if required, add yellow ochre; and to increase the richness of the color, you may substitute vermilion for red ochre, and add stone yellow instead of ochre.

Good Drying Black.—Put some lamp-black into an iron ladle, and place it over the fire till it becomes red-hot, and when the smoke is disengaged from it, take it from the fire and extinguish it upon the slab, or mix with some boiled oil; add a proportion of burnt white vitriol. If a jet black is required, add a little Prussian blue.

Another.—Mix drop black in gold-size and turps, to dry quickly, one-third size.

Another.—Mix drop black in oil and turps.

Lead.—This is a mixture of lamp-black and white lead, with a little litharge.

Chocolate.—Mix lamp-black and Venetian red with a little red lead, or litharge, to harden the color, and give a drying quality. The colors must be ground, and mixed with boiled oil and a little turps.

Dark Red, for common purposes.—Mix English Venetian red in boiled oil, with a little red lead and litharge to give a drying quality.

Lighter Red.—Mix together equal parts of Venetian red and red lead, in boiled oil and turps.

To Imitate Vermilion.—Grind together in oil red lead and rose pink.

Deep Red.—Mix in oil vermilion, with a dust of Venetian red or red lead.

Orange.—Mix red lead and French yellow with linseed oil and turps.

Unfading Orange.—This is a mixture of orange lead (orpiment) and French or stone yellow, oil and turps.

An excellent bright Yellow for Floors, &c.—White lead and linseed oil, mixed with some French yellow, and a little chrome yellow to brighten it; some red lead, burnt white vitriol and litharge, added, to give it a very drying quality. This color, mixed with equal parts of boiled oil and turpentine, and used very thin.

Light Pine.—Mix spruce ochre with white lead and umber.

Dark Yellow.—Mix French yellow in boiled oil, adding to it a little red lead and litharge, to give the paint a drying quality

Light Yellow.—This is a mixture of French yellow and white lead, with oil and turps.

Another.—French yellow, white lead, and read lead.

Another.—Grind raw terradasienna in turps and linseed oil; mix with white lead. If the color is required of a warmer cast, add a little burnt terradasienna ground in turps.

Free Stone.—A mixture of red lead, Venetian red, French yellow, and lamp-black, varying the shade according to taste, with linseed oil and turps.

Dark Lead-color, in Oil.—Use white, black, and indigo.

Stone-color.—Yellow ochre, umber, and white lead.

Olive Green.—A suitable, cheap, and handsome color for outside work, such as doors, carts, wagons, &c.

Grind separately Prussian blue and French yellow in boiled oil; then mix to the tint required with a little burnt white vitriol, to act as a drier.

Another.—This is a mixture of Prussian blue, French yellow, a small portion of Turkey umber, and a little burnt vitriol. Ground the same way.

Another, in Oil.—Mix Prussian blue and chrome yellow. Ground the same.

Another Shade.—A mixture of Prussian blue and French yellow, with a small quantity of white lead and Turkey umber; add burnt white vitriol. Ground the same.

Another, light.—White, mixed with verdigris. A variety of shades may be obtained by using blue and yellow with white lead.

Another, grass.—Yellow, mixed with verdigris.

Another.—Mix one pound of verdigris with two pounds of white lead. Walnut oil is the best for this purpose.

Another, Olive.—Black and blue mixed with yellow, in such quantities as to obtain the colors or shades required. For distemper, use indigo and yellow pink mixed with whiting or white lead powder.

Another, invisible, for outside work.—Mix lamp-black and French yellow with burnt white vitriol. These colors mix in boiled oil. Burnt vitriol is the best drier for greens, as it is powerful and colorless, and consequently will not injure the color.

Brigh Varnish-Green, for Inside Blinds, Fenders, &c.— The work must first be painted once over with a light lead color, and when dry, grind some white lead in spirits of turpentine; afterwards take about one-third in bulk of verdigris, which has been ground stiff in linseed oil; then mix them both together, and put into it a little resin varnish, sufficient only to bind the color. When this is hard, which will be the case in fifteen minutes, pour into the color some resin varnish to give it a good gloss. Then go over the work a second time, and, if required, a third time. Thus you will have a cheap and beautiful green with a high polish. It possesses a very drying quality, as the work may be completed in a few hours. The tint may be varied according to taste, by substituting mineral green for verdigris; and if a bright grass-green is required, add a little Dutch pink to the mixture.

N. B.—This color must be used when quite warm, to give the varnish an uniform extension.

Pea Green.—Take one pound of genuine mineral green, one pound of the precipitate of copper, one pound and a half of blue verditer, three pounds of white lead, three ounces of sugar of lead, and three ounces of burnt white vitriol. Mix the whole of these ingredients in linseed oil, and grind them quite fine. It will produce a bright mineral pea-green paint, preserve a blue tint, and keep any length of time in any climate, without injury, by putting water over it. To use this color for house or ship painting, take one pound of the green paint with some pale boiled oil, mix them well together, and this will produce a strong pea-green paint. The tint may be altered at pleasure, by adding a proportionate quantity of white lead to the green, which may be ground in linseed oil, and thinned with spirits of turpentine for use. It may also be used for painting Venetian window-blinds, by adding white lead, and mixing the color with boiled oil. For all the aforesaid preparations it will retain a blue tint, which is very desirable.

Compound Greens.—This is a mixture of whiting, indigo, and Dutch pink, the intensity of which may be increased or diminished by the addition of blue or yellow. These mixtures will not admit of any fixed rules in regard to the quantity of the matters used in their composition. They must depend on the taste of the artist, and the tone he is desirous of giving to the color.

Painting on Glass.—One ounce of clear resin; melt it in an iron vessel; when all is melted, let it cool a little, but not harden; then add oil of turpentine sufficient to keep it in a liquid state. When cold, use it with ground colors in oil.

To Imitate Ground Glass.—Two ounces of spirits of salts, two ounces of oil of vitriol, one ounce of sulphate of copper, one ounces of gum arabic, mixed together, and dabbed on with a brush.

Another.—Dab your squares regularly over with putty; when dry, go over them again, the imitation will be executed.

Another.—Mix Epsom salts with porter, and apply it with a brush.

To Paint in Imitation of Ground Glass.—Grind and mix white lead in three-fourths of boiled oil, and one-fourth of spirits of turpentine; and to give the mixture a very drying quality, add sufficient quantities of burnt white vitriol and sugar of lead. The color must be made exceedingly thin, and put on the panes of glass with a large painting-brush in as even a manner as possible. When a number of the panes are thus painted, take a dry duster, quite new, dab the ends of the bristles on the glass in quick succession, till you give it an uniform appearance; repeat this operation till the work appears very soft, and it will then appear like ground glass. When the windows require fresh painting, get the old coat off first by using strong pearl-ash water. This application requires but little labor.

Quick Drying Color.—Mix the color in two-thirds of turpentine, and one of gold-size; then varnish when dry.

To Prepare Oil for Walls.—The oil should be boiling. To make the oil drying, add half an ounce of litharge to a quart of linseed oil.

Hard Drying Paint.—Grind Venetian red, or any other color you think proper, in boiled oil; then thin it with black japan. It will dry very hard for counter-tops, &c.

Carnation Color, in Oil.—A mixture of lake and white.

Fawn Color.—White lead, stone ochre, and vermilion.

First coat for Sheet Iron.—Use yellow ochre in oil or Venetian red; a little white lead may be added.

To paint a Bronze.—Grind good black with chrome yellow and boiled oil; apply it with a brush, and when nearly dry use the bronze powder at certain parts, and the edges also; the effect will be a brassy hue.

Lead Color for Iron, &c.—Take litharge and place it over a fire in an iron ladle; sprinkle over it flour of brimstone. To turn it dark grind it in oil. It dries quick, and stands well in any weather.

A good Imitation of Gold.—Mix white lead, chrome yellow, and burnt sienna, until the proper shade is obtained.

Painter's Cream.—Which preserves the color and freshness of work when it is allowed to remain unfinished; use as varnish. Make it as follows: One ounce of mastic finely powdered, and dissolve it over a gentle fire in six ounces of clear nut-oil. Put it into a marble mortar with five drachms of powdered sugar of lead, stir all together with a wooden pestle, adding water in small quantities till it has the appearance of cream, and refuses more water so as to mix freely.

For cleaning Stone Pavement, Steps at Hall Doors, &c.—Boil together one pint of white size, with the same quantity of stone-blue water, four cakes of pipe-clay, four table spoonfuls of whiting in one gallon of water. Wash the stones slightly with this, and when dry, rub them with a flannel and brush.

To clean Marble.—Mix a bullock's gall with four ounces of soap-lees and two ounces of turpentine, add pipe-clay, and make it into a paste. Apply it to the marble, and let it remain twenty-four hours; rub it off, and if not clean, repeat it till it is.

Another.—Apply muriatic acid; if too strong, it will take off the polish. Polish again with felt and tripoli, or putty powder, and use water with either.

To clean Alabaster.—Pumice-stone, powdered fine and mixed with verjuice. Let it stand for three hours, and rub it over; wash it with a linen cloth and water; rub dry with clean linen rags.

To make Chrome Yellow.—One pound of dry white lead, ground in water, two ounces of sugar of lead, one ounce of cromate of potash. The two last dissolved in one pint of boiling water, and poured upon the lead. When settled, pour off the water and dried.

Tar-Paint for Fences, Roofs, &c.—Common tar mixed with whiting, Venetian red, or French yellow, according to the color required. This should be warmed in a large iron kettle in the open air, and applied with a large painting-brush. It is an excellent preservative of the wood, and looks well for rough work.

Paint-Dryers; Litharge.—This is a useful dryer, and may be used in all kinds of paints, except greens and very delicate colors.

White Vitriol or Copperas.—This turns into water, especially when used in black paints, and is almost useless for any color till the water of crystallization is evaporated, and then it becomes a powerful dryer, and may be used for every delicate color, as it is perfectly transparent; but when used in its raw state in white paint, has the effect of turning it yellow.

Sugar of Lead.—This is a very useful and transparent dryer; not so powerful as white vitriol, but it may be used with it to advantage.

To Prepare Damp Walls for Painting.—One pound of good glue dissolved in one gallon of water, and thickened with red lead; to be brushed on while hot.

To Repair Broken Walls.—Use plaster of Paris and white-house sand, in nearly equal quantities, mixed with water.

To Dry Damp Walls.—To make them fit for papering, wash the damp wall with sulphuric acid, by which the deliquescent salts are decomposed, it then becomes dry.

To Remove Paint and Oil from Boards.—Mix together soap-lees and fuller's-earth; rub it in and let it dry; afterwards scour it with soft soap, sand, and hot water.

For Whiting Ceilings in Distemper.—Half a pound of roach-alum dissolved in hot water, two pounds of selica, and six pounds of whiting, for six ceilings, twenty feet by sixteen. This mixture will give time for the workman to execute his work properly.

Quantity of Color to be used.—For first coat mix one pound for twelve yards of mahogany-color; for oak, &c., double the quantity; for drabs and stone-colors, the same quantity.

Quantity of Varnish to be used.—One pint to sixteen square yards, for first coat.

For Cleaning Oil Paintings, Wainscoting, or Furniture.—Smash or grate into clean water raw potatoes, sufficient to form a thin paste, add fine powdered pumice-stone or fine sand, and with a sponge well clean the work, then finish with water and a cloth. When dry, polish or varnish may be applied.

To Kill Smoke on Walls.—Walls, if almost black, and are very smoky, must be brushed as clean as possible with a broom, and in order to kill the smoke, wash them over with strong pearl-ash or soda-water, and immediately rinse them with clear water before the pearl-ash is dry. When dry, give them a thin coat of fresh slacked lime, with a good proportion of alum dissolved in hot water and mixed with it. The work should be finished with whiting and London size. Be careful not to apply the size-distemper till the lime-wash is dry, as the latter will destroy the strength of the size if they come in contact while wet.

For Smoky Mantel-pieces, &c.—Mix a strong solution of alum and water, and apply it hot; when dry, sand paper it, and give it a coat of paint.

To Prepare Smoky Rooms for Painting.—If there is a smoky gloss on the part intended to be painted, rub it off with sand-paper, and whitewash over with newly-slacked lime. When this is dry, brush it off clean, and well scrub the work with strong pearl-ash water, and afterwards rinse it well with clear water; finish it by giving it a coat of weak size, with a little white lead powder mixed with it, or dissolve alum in hot water and brush on.

To Clean Oil Paintings if Smoked, Dull, or Dirty.—Dissolve a little common salt with stale urine and a grated potato mixed in them; rub them over with a woollen cloth till you think them clean, then with a sponge wash them over with clear water, then dry them, and rub them over with a clean cloth.

To Whiten Linseed Oil.—Shake up daily two ounces of litharge in a gallon of oil and eight ounces of spirits of turpentine, for fifteen days, afterwards let it settle three days. Pour off the clear part into a shallow vessel, and place it in the sun three days to whiten and clear it.

To Cure Damp Walls.—Boil two ounces of grease with two quarts of tar, for nearly twenty minutes, in an iron vessel, and having ready pounded glass one pound, slacked lime two pounds; well dried in an iron pot, and sifted through a flour sieve. Add some of the lime to the tar and glass, to make it the thickness of a thin paste sufficient to cover a square foot at a time, as it hardens so quick. Apply it about an eighth of an inch thick.

To Prepare Wood and Brick Work from damp weather.—Take three pecks of lime slacked in the air, two ditto of wood ashes, and one peck of fine sand. Sift them fine, and add linseed oil sufficient to use with a paint-brush; thin the first coat; use it as thick as it will work the second coat. Grind it fine or beat it in a trough, and it is a good composition.

Putty for Repairing Broken Walls.—The best putty for walls is composed of equal parts of whiting and plaster of Paris, as it quickly hardens. The walls may be immediately colored upon it. Some painters use whiting mixed with size; but this is not good, as it rises above the surface of the walls, and shows in patches when the work is finished. Lime must not be used as a putty to repair walls, as it will destroy almost every color it comes in contact with.

ART OF IMITATING OAK, MAHOGANY, SATIN WOOD, WALNUT, ROSE WOOD, AND MAPLE.

Oak is preferable to other imitations for outside work, on doors and shutters, where a show of strength and durability is required. As it is capable of great and pleasing variety and contrast, skill and taste are only to be properly attained in this, as in other imitations, by a careful study of the best specimens of the natural wood. The lightest parts of oak, called the flowers, should be carefully studied, with a view to color the ground properly. The light buff color here seen, is made with raw umber and white, and sometimes tinged with Indian red, according to the character of the wood, as age changes the tints of oak materially. The ground, however, should be always light in color, because it can be easily remedied in shade by glazing. This groundwork, in all cases, should be quite hard, smooth, and clean, as much of the beauty of the work depends upon it. It is best made, as before noted, of white, tinted with raw umber, taking care to make it a light color.

Many varieties of brushes and tools are used: the copper-bound, ground-coating brush, steel-combs, of extra fine, fine, graduated, middling, and coarse teeth, from one inch to six inches wide; leather-combs of various widths; horn-combs, of different fineness of teeth and widths; sable and hog-hair overgrains; badger blenders, knotted and flat; camel's-hair and hog-hair dab-tools; hog-hair blenders and flogger; wash-leather, cork-stump, oak-striper, sable and camel's-hair pencils, large and small fitches, &c.

They also prepare their color variously, but the following recipe will be found useful for a megilp:

Take eight ounces of rotten-stone, and eight ounces of sugar of lead, and grind them together as stiffly as possible in linseed oil. Then take sixteen ounces of white wax, and melt it gradually in an earthen pipkin. When quite fluid, pour in carefully eight ounces of spirits of turpentine. Mix this well with the wax: when well mixed, pour the contents of the pipkin on the grinding-stone to get cold; when cold, grind the rotten-stone and sugar of lead as above, with the wax, and it will form an excellent megilp, which will keep a long time if protected from dust. When required to be used, it is to be taken out with a pallet-knife on the stone or pallet-board, and tempered with boiled oil.

The first operation for the graining, is to spread the megilp evenly and thinly upon the work, with the copper-bound brush. A few minutes after, take the widest and most separated tooth comb—some use the leather combs, and others the horn—and holding it firmly, draw it over the work, making the grain slantwise or wavy, as the work may require. This large tooth comb will take up but little of the megilp, spreading it, making it come up between the teeth in thicker streaks. It is better not to go over more than a yard square at one time, as the megilp dries quickly, and when dry is unmanageable. After the large comb is passed over, it is to be followed by the next size, tremulously drawn over the whole work, rather towards one side, bearing more heavily on some parts than others. This will break up the first lines, and is to be followed up by the finer combs progressively, using the finer combs to produce the grains nearest the heart of the tree.

Having used the combs, take a piece of wash-leather, and, doubling it to a point, take out the lights or flowers of the oak, and if these are wanted fine, go over it again with the wash-leather, over the end of a stick, or use the cork-stump. The work is sometimes left here, but can be sensibly improved by the use of the flogger, to break up the lines, and also the oak bander, which is used as a top-grainer, straitly over the work with thin megilp. If darker touches are required, they are best made with the megilp, ground with Vandyke brown, instead of the rotten-stone; and if the work needs darkening, a little raw or burnt umber should be mixed with the megilp and glazed over it.

In forming joints or panels of this wood, flowers or lights, well formed, should be carefully drawn next each other, and as few knots as convenient introduced, nor any very dark or glazed panels along side the unglazed ones, to make the others glare and stand out too much.

If you wish to form a join, lay a straight-edge along the edge, guarding its ends with paper, and, holding it firmly, draw the second fine comb along the edge sharply, keeping the end close against it. This will form a good join. Sometimes the large comb is used on both sides of the panel, letting the grain meet in the centre, the fine combs following with a wavy motion in the same direction, and the remainder of the work finished as before. In this way many varieties of work can be introduced, copying the best specimens of the natural wood you can obtain.

Be careful to wash the brushes and tools well from the megilp, so as to keep them clean, especially the teeth of the combs. Dry the horn combs, and keep them wrapped in wash-leather.

Oak in Distemper is made with raw and burnt umber and Vandyke brown, ground in water, and tempered with old beer. Of late years, Mr. Stephens, of London, a celebrated chemist, has prepared chemical paste colors, which attach themselves firmly to the ground, and are found useful in indoor work, as they are prepared just the requisite tints of oak, maple, mahogany, and satin wood colors. The ground for distemper oak is similar to that of oak, except that if it be required to make it darker, you must have a little Indian red added to your ground-color, as you cannot depend on your glazing to alter it.

The ground must be perfectly clean and dry—free from any grease spots or finger marks, as the color will not hold on them.

When your ground is clean and dry, take some of your paste-color, or raw umber and sienna, ground thickly in water, and put it on your pallet-board, and, after thinning it a little with the beer, with your copper-bound brush working it through the color thoroughly, until it is full of the color, draw it diagonally and wavily across the work, in such a way as somewhat to imitate the combing in oil. Then with the flogger lightly beat it with the points of the hairs, the reverse way to that in which the color is laid on, quickly, and with a light hand, varying and turning the hand to correspond with the grain put on. By this time, the work will have become tachy or nearly dry, when the flowers or lights are to be taken out with a damp wash-leather, folded to a point, or over the end of a stick, or with a cork-stump, as described in the oil-graining.

It is well to do this with spirit, and not attempt too large a surface at once, that it may remain sufficiently damp to finish it together. As soon as it is dry, with a sable-pencil filled with umber and Vandyke brown, diluted with beer, put in the dark veins that cross the grain. When the panel is finished with damp washleather, wipe the edges clean where the adjoining work has been touched, and proceed to the next panel, wiping the damp cloth over it to clean it, and enable the color to take on it; then proceed as above, varying your work according to fancy. If a knot be required in the work, make it small on the sides of the panels or stiles, by putting the wash-leather over the end of the fore-finger, and placing it where the knot is wanted: holding it firmly in one spot and turning it around, will take the color off as is desired—the lights above and below to be taken out with the folded wash-leather, and the whole blended with the badger-brush. A join is made against or across the work, along the straight-edge, with the flogger, used as the comb in oil. When the panels are finished, draw the damp wash-leather over the finger, and wipe off the color which may have touched beyond them in finishing the panels, using the straight-edge where it is necessary to define the end or edge of the work. The stiles may then be similarly grained, varying the ornaments and grain, so as to produce a pleasing contrast. When the whole work is finished, it must be varnished, and if it needs retouching, to darken it, or vein it, it can be done just before the varnishing, with the sable-pencil, as noted above.

As this is intended for learners, it may be well to re capitulate some of the leading directions.

1st. The ground must be dry and clean, wiped over with the damp wash-leather.

2d. Have all the colors you may require, with your pallet, wash-leather, cork-stump, brushes, &c., ready for use, as the color dries too rapidly to allow any time to go for them.

3d. To have the appearance of the work required formed in the mind, so that you can work quickly and decidedly. If you are not capable to do that, you must have a pattern before you.

4th. Never prepare too much at one time, nor endeavor to patch or mend: if it does not suit, rub all out and commence again.

5th. In pencilling the fine veins, do not have the color too wet, lest it run on the ground and drag on the graining, spreading over the work. Let these dark lines be always wavy.

Some grainers, after grinding the color in beer, mix a little soap, wax, and turpentine, to hinder its quick drying, and make it work smoothly; but it clogs the flogger, and thereby mars the work. Some, before graining, beat soap into a lather, and brush it thickly over the work, to make the color work softer and more pleasant. Yet the fine ground-color, as first described, is the best and most easy with a little practice. An old style, now exploded, was to put the color on thickly, and take out the lights with dilute muriatic acid, grain over it, and then, brushing it smartly with a duster, the parts touched by the acid came off. It never makes the fine work as the regular way; yet nature is the best guide, and will direct the judgment and skill as the best action, according to its location and character.

Satin Wood is principally used on inside work and on panels, the stiles alongside generally grained in rose wood. The ground for this wood is a light buff, and, when dry and perfectly clean, paint it smoothly over with Oxford ochre, finely ground in strong beer. Then, with a fine dab-tool, wipe out the lights from top to bottom, or lengthwise of the work, in a free and careless manner. Then soften the edges with the badger blender, working it transversely. When the work is quite dry, mix raw sienna and raw umber, finely ground with the beer, and dilute it, and with your sable top-grainer pass lightly over the work in a wavy direction, and use the blender immediately, brushing it more upon the light parts to take off the grain. When dry and varnished, it will be finished.

Mahogany Color.—The ground should be prepared with Venetian red and white. The color to be used on outside or exposed work is burnt sienna, finely ground in oil; rose pink for the light veining-ground, in boiled oil and spirits of turpentine; the dark veining, Vandyke brown, also ground in boiled oil and spirits of turpentine. Remember to make the tint of the ground light colored. This ground is first covered with a thin coat of the burnt sienna, heightened with the rose pink, diluted with japan and spirits of turpentine, and if the tint suit, the mottling must be wiped out with the dab-tool, after the manner of the satin wood just described;

after softening with the badger-brush, the light veins then passed over with the sable top-grainer, made almost wholly with rose pink; and, ultimately, the fine dark veins, grained over with the hog-hair top-grainer: the color, made of thin Vandyke brown, tempered as before with japan and spirits of turpentine, and it is ready for the varnish.

Mahogany in Distemper, is worked with the same colors, ground in water and tempered with old beer. If the work requires heightening, add a little orange chrome yellow to the ground-color, and proceed with the work somewhat after the manner described in the satin wood directions, except that the panels are usually worked so as to show a diagonal heart or crotch, which is frequently observed in the natural veneers. The stiles are to be finished more straightly, and not so deep in color. A close study of the best veneers of this beautiful wood, will enable the workman to make passable imitations of it. It is, when dry, ready for the varnish.

Walnut is worked with crotches or veining, similar to the mahogany; making the ground with ochre, Indian red, umber, and white. The megilp, as described under the oak heading, is prepared with Vandyke brown; and for the darker shades, fine ivory-black; the wiping out and blending to resemble that in the mahogany; the fine dark veins of ivory-black, to be lightly and wavily drawn over the work after it is blended. It is then ready for the varnish.

Rose Wood is of a great variety of tints. The ground is formed of vermilion, lake, and white; the veins formed, as above, with Vandyke brown and ivory-black. Spread nearly over the work, with a hog-hair over-grain, lightly veining every part of it; after which, as in distemper oak, the color is to be flogged against the grain. Then, with the cork-stump, or the wash-leather, drawn over the end of a stick, the lights are to be wiped out in an elongated manner, as if caused by small knots; then, with the Vandyke brown and ivory-black, and sable-pencil or fine tool, put strong and free touches under those lights. Thin fine veins are to be made with the sable over-grains, and the dark color over the whole work, and lightly blended, after which it is ready for the varnish.

Maple is painted on the same ground as oak, with burnt umber, mixed with the beer, or with Stephen's prepared color. The color is brushed thinly over the ground, and then the surface is grained all over with the hog-hair top-grainer, after which a fine sable over-grainer is used to put therein a light wavy touch, in nearly the same general direction. The work is then to be lightly blended, and if bird's eyes are required, they are made with a sable-pencil, worked on the point in the darker parts of the work. If no bird's eyes are put in the work, it is to be flogged against the grain, as before described, and some light veining passed over, when it is ready for the varnish. The foregoing directions will serve a workman of taste to imitate almost any woods, taking care to study the ground in the light parts of the wood.

Marble Imitation.—The white or Parian marble is most easily imitated with the China white varnish paint, not glossed, and figures and niches shaded in it with blue black and Vandyke brown. Cipolin, or white-veined marble, is usually imitated in oil-color, or perhaps might be more perfectly white with the varnish white, tempered with white wax. Its first broad veins, seen in the semi-transparent surface, are of a reddish gray, formed with some white, blue black, and Indian red.

Veins of marble, of all kinds, run similar to thin streams of water, as they would show on an inclined plane, as the top of a table raised by one corner; which, if they commence regularly, soon alter their course—now forming a star, thence spreading with finer threads; others join into a thick vein, and again separate, yet all coursing without sudden break to the bottom. Following such general courses, the first broad vein must be scumbled in, like thick branches. Over these, and following the same direction, the darker veins, with black added, are next drawn, a little zig-zag in their course; and again another fine vein, made richer with lake, and darkened with Vandyke brown, still more wavily drawn with the fine sable-pencil. The whole must then be lightly and carefully blended; the veining-color may be mixed with japan and spirits, to facilitate its drying. When dry, it must be varnished with the lightest copal.

Marbling Walls.—Walls may be imitated in distemper or size, by using fine whiting, tempered with glue size, and lamp or blue black, Indian red and slip blue, tempered with old beer. A similar process is to be followed, taking care not to wet over a square yard at one time, and carefully damping the edges of the finished parts, so as to join the work properly, and coursing over the work, before blending, a thin white vein. Other wall marbling may be done by making a fawn size-color of yellow ochre, white, and a little Indian red. Have some clear white and Indian red ready, and commence by dabbing on with freedom the fawn color, in various sized and shaped spots, with the Indian red and a little white mixed; fill all the spaces between the spots of fawn color. After these are blended, follow over their edges with a fine sable-pencil, with the white and pure red. When these are lightly blended, the work is done.

Sienna Marble.—The ground for this is yellow ochre, a little white and chrome yellow, mixed together ground in oil, and tempered with japan and spirits. The shadings are yellow ochre and white, raw and burnt sienna, ground and tempered with japan and spirits, made to run into each other, being painted thinly over the ground with a brush for each color, and blended together. While these are yet wet, the first veins are put in with a large sable-pencil, made of Venetian red and Prussian blue, lines running in the same direction and lightly blended in. Those nearest the surface are formed of lake, Indian red, and blue, and follow the same general direction, and must be drawn with care and spirit. After the work is dry, the shading can be deepened with a glazing of raw and burnt sienna, and the darker veins run over with lake and Prussian blue. Specimens of the natural marble are the best guides.

Black and Gold Marble, is imitated by painting the ground a good black; then, with a thick mixture of yellow ochre, white, and a little vermilion, imitating the gold-color, put on in masses in various parts of the work with a small brush, quite full of color, dabbed on, and from these spots small veins must be wavily drawn, like thick and thin threads variously, in one general direction, and sometimes a clear, white vein crosses them diagonally, keeping the same general course. When dry, varnish it. Small specimens are sometimes produced beautifully by putting on strips of gold and silver-leaf, painting the black over, and wiping out the bright veins with a stump and bodkin, and then varnishing.

Verd-antique.—Have pure China white, ground fine in japan and spirits, Prussian blue the same, and also raw sienna. Over a black ground, paint the white, with the copper-bound brush, in shady, diagonal stripes over the work. Then, with the wash-leather over the finger, by turning it firmly and quickly around, imitate the shells and other fossils in various parts; with an overgrainer pass over the white, to draw out faint lines over the black. After it is dry, glaze some parts with Prussian blue, and others with raw sienna, and leave some black and white. The thicker veins may be touched with the sable-pencil with Prussian blue, and over the strong lights small dark veins. When dry, the final glazing is to be made with Prussian blue and raw sienna mixed, which will form over the work a fine warm green. When dry, it is ready for the varnish.

Porphyry.—The ground is white, mixed with Indian red, and heightend with vermilion. The spots are produced upon it by tinting white with the ground-color, into which the copper-bound brush may be dipped, and well worked in the color, then carefully drawn over the edge of a pallet-knife to discharge the color. Then, holding the handle firmly between the palms of the hands, turn it around swiftly in the pot, until scarcely any color is thrown from it. Then, holding an old knife over the work, strike the copper binding of the brush upon it, and it will spot the work in points. When dry, it must again be sprinkled with a little darker color, made so with Indian red mixed in with a little white, and put on in clouds on parts of the work. The last coat is done with very fine spots of white, sprinkled in the same way from a brush wrung out as dry as possible, and the stick held a yard or two from the work, on which the brush is knocked. A thin white vein or two in the corner completes the work, and when dry, it is ready for the varnish.

Graniting is done in the same manner, substituting a light gray ground, and spotting with blue black and white mixed; the next coat, ivory-black and a little white; and the last white, with a little blue black mixed.

These directions may suffice to guide the workman in imitating any Marbles, yet Nature must be the best guide, and as many specimens obtained as he can procure.

DIRECTIONS FOR PAINTING SAIL-CLOTH, TO MAKE IT PLIANT, WATER-PROOF, AND DURABLE.

In order to do this, you must boil ninety-six pounds of English ochre with boiled oil, and add to it sixteen pounds of black paint. Dissolve a pound of yellow soap in two gallons of water on the fire, and mix it while hot with the paint. Lay this composition, without wetting it, upon the canvas as stiff as can conveniently be done with a brush, so as to form a smooth surface; the next day, or the second day after, lay on a second coat of ochre and black, with a very little soap; allow this coat a day to dry, and then finish the canvas with black paint.

Directions for making a Varnish which will protect Glass from the rays of the sun.

To do this properly, reduce a quantity of gum tragacanth to fine powder, and let it dissolve for twenty-four hours in white of eggs well beat up; then rub it gently on the glass with a brush.

www.ingramcontent.com/pod-product-compliance
Lightning Source LLC
Chambersburg PA
CBHW020826230426
43666CB00007B/1113